GADFLY ON THE WALL
A PUBLIC SCHOOL TEACHER SPEAKS OUT ON
RACISM AND REFORM

GADFLY ON THE WALL

A PUBLIC SCHOOL TEACHER SPEAKS OUT ON RACISM AND REFORM

STEVEN SINGER

GARN PRESS
NEW YORK, NY

Published by Garn Press, LLC
New York, NY
www.garnpress.com

Book and cover design by Benjamin J. Taylor/Garn Press
Cover Image by Pana Vasquez/Unsplash

First Edition, November, 2017

Library of Congress Control Number: 2017948574

Publisher's Cataloging-in-Publication Data

Names: Singer, Steven.
Title: Gadfly on the Wall: A Public School Teacher Speaks Out on Racism and Reform / Steven Singer.
Description: First edition. | New York : Garn Press, 2017. | Includes bibliographical references.
Identifiers: LCCN 2017948574 | ISBN 978-1-942146-67-4 (pbk.) | ISBN 978-1-942146-68-1 (Kindle ebook)
Subjects: LCSH: Racism. | School choice. | Charter schools--United States. | Educational tests and measurement. | Teaching. | BISAC: SOCIAL SCIENCE / Discrimination & Race Relations. | EDUCATION / Education Policy & Reform/Charter Schools. | EDUCATION / Standards (Incl. Common Core). | EDUCATION / Professional Development. | EDUCATION / Aims & Objectives.
Classification: LCC LB1027.9 .S45 2017 (print) | LCC LB1027.9 (ebook) | DDC 371.3--dc23.
LC record available at https://lccn.loc.gov/2017948574

CONTENTS

To Elisha and Desi

"To sting people and whip them into a fury, all in the service of truth."

Socrates

FOREWORD

YOHURU R. WILLIAMS

Merriam Webster defines a gadfly as "a person who stimulates or annoys other people especially by persistent criticism." Over the past four years blogger Steven Singer has certainly fit this bill. In his biting commentary on issues related to teaching, education reform, poverty, and racial and gender inequality, he has been both a voice of truth and a stinging critic pointing out the deep flaws in the logic and propaganda floated by the apostles of privatization and corporate education reform. In the process, he has managed to build a national following for his popular blog post with scores of admirers on Social Media.

The tag line of Steven's blog "To sting people and whip them into a fury, all in the service of truth" evokes the image of the original gadfly Socrates, who was forced to drink hemlock of course for his bruising critique of Athenian Society, which, much like our own, had become mired in shadows and half-truths. Socrates recognized the need to help the Athenians, to borrow a contemporary phrase, "stay woke" in the defense of the Republic. As he explained to his accusers, "the state is a great and noble steed who is tardy in his motions owing to his very size, and requires to be stirred into life." It is an apt comparison for Steven, whose fearless questioning of the status quo is its own form of Socratic inquiry. He always seems to ask more questions than he answers. There is, nevertheless, a method and message in his approach. Only by interrogating the evidence, questioning motives, and asking the difficult questions can we ever hope to distinguish fact from fiction. The strong positions he has taken, especially on issues related to corporate education reform, reflect his relentless probing and prodding of the false narratives meant to mask efforts to dismantle public education.

There is a folksy quality to his writing, meant to disarm as it informs. I remember the first blog of his I read in September of 2014, where he compared efforts by political officials attempting to justify cuts in education spending in Pennsylvania to "a bully shouting, 'Why are you hitting yourself!?' as he slaps a little kid in the face with the child's own hands!" I laughed until it hurt – not from the obvious humor but because of its stark truth.

I met Steven in person almost a year later in the summer of 2015 at the second annual Badass Teachers Association (BATS) Conference in Washington, DC. Although we had been acquainted in cyberspace, I fully admit to being a bit surprised when I finally came face to face with the quiet and otherwise unassuming man behind the provocative blog posts. As we exchanged greetings and posed for the obligatory selfie, I asked him what drove his passion for activism. He paused for a moment, clumsily adjusting his glasses, deep in thought.

"The same thing that drives us all," he finally responded, "I'm a parent and a teacher in that order. There is no more important fight." I was not surprised by his answer, like thousands of other activists in the effort to save public education, Steven was drafted into the movement by the assault on public education, and his activism has not been without consequences.

Unapologetic and relentless in his critiques, Steven has endured his fair share of animosity. At the writing of this Foreword in October 2017, he was blocked from the Social Media website Facebook for posting a blog entitled "School Choice is a Lie. It Does Not Mean More Options. It Means Less." In a subsequent blog, a brilliant indictment of Facebook and censorship in social media, cloaked in a series of seemingly harmless questions, Steven acknowledges, "I've pissed off a lot of people in three years." The present volume, a collection of some of his most popular and provocative posts, provides a glimpse into the mind of the gadfly. Through his thoughtful, reflective writing and activism, he has enlightened thousands and helped to force conversations around critical issues that many sadly still take for granted.

Yohuru R. Williams
Professor of History, Dean of the College of Arts and Sciences at the University of St. Thomas, Minnesota

FOREWORD

DENISHA JONES

I noticed early on in my work as an education activist that the movement was making a fatal flaw. As we organized to make people aware of the dangers of corporate education reform, we failed to make explicit the ideologies that allowed privatizers to push test-based accountability and school choice scams. We focused on their greed and quest to maximize profits without calling out other motives. And when others called us out we went on the defensive instead of realizing that they were right and we needed to rethink our strategy. Some of us realized our mistake and shifted our approach to right the wrong, but others insisted that their approach was best, and as a result the movement splintered.

In many ways, we were all still working for the same end goal, to stop the spread of the global education reform movement (GERM) from turning public education into a privatized commodity, but our methods diverged. On one side were those who insisted on a color-blind, race-neutral approach, and the other side were those who knew that we must center racism and white supremacy in all efforts to resist the attack on public education. To take a race-neutral approach meant we would ignore how racism and white supremacy are ingrained within the founding of America's public schools. Without this foundational knowledge, many activists fell into the trap of only recognizing injustice when it happened to *their* family and *their* community.

When the Common Core State Standards were adopted by more than 40 states and new tests were developed to measure how well the standards were being taught, many parents and teachers felt this was an overreach by the federal government. Anti-Common Core groups sprung up around the country, and the growing vocal opposition caused some states to withdraw from implementing the standards. Where was their outrage when schools in poor black communities were being closed and replaced with charters? Many failed to make the connection because they did not center how racism and white supremacy operates in schools that serve other people's children. Charters and under-prepared-temporary-saviors-turned-educators (aka Teach For America corps members) were okay for kids in "urban" schools, but as long as they did not move into their community, those anti-Common Core activists were silent.

This silence allowed the privatizers to co-opt the language of the civil rights movements and convince low-income parents of color that "school choice" and vouchers were going to save them from "failing" schools. Instead of investing in public schools that were set up to fail, they could let businesses come in and create for-profit management companies to run charter schools. Those who took a race-neutral approach did not pay attention to this or worry about it because it was not happening to them. The national standards and new tests were their only concern. But as "school choice" and other corporate reform scams gained support it became clear that resistance would be futile if we did not address the bigger picture.

As I continued to work within various education activist groups, we chose to center racism and white supremacy in our fight to stop the privatization of public education. Organizations like the Badass Teachers Association, United Opt Out, and Save Our Schools worked together to fight for social justice and expose how high stakes standardized testing is rooted in eugenics and white supremacy ideologies, how school closings were fueled by racism, and how attacks on teacher unions negatively impacted teachers of color. As a result of our efforts, people like Steven Singer were drawn to us, and it turns out we were fortunate to receive him and his talents.

I remember the first time I read his blog, where he called himself and other white people racist. I was immediately reminded of an analogy Dr. Beverly Tatum gives in her groundbreaking book *Why are all the Black Kids Sitting Together in the Cafeteria* where she compares racism to a moving walkway. Active racists walk along the moving walkway promoting racism, passive racists stand on the moving walkway neither supporting nor fighting racism but letting it move them along nonetheless, and anti-racists walk backward on the moving walkway resisting racism. Steven was acknowledging that as a white person he and many others are Tatum's version of passive racists, but I reminded him that through his writing and actions he was working to be an anti-racist. But to do that he and others need to recognize that passive racism is real and is often cloaked in color-blind and race-neutral beliefs. Acknowledging how racism is a pervasive ingredient to our society is a necessary first step to resisting corporate education reform.

Bloggers get to use their voice to educate readers about issues they may not know are even happening. Sometimes the goal is to entertain, but often we try and persuade people and coax them to action with thoughtful and even provocative prose. Steven takes this one step further by calling himself a gadfly, a person who disrupts the status quo through criticisms directed at authority figures. His work not only serves as an inspiration to fellow activists and a source of knowledge for newbies, but more importantly it is a direct challenge to all who think they can buy our public education system and use it to maintain white supremacy. Whether it is challenging the current administration to allow refugees into his school or calling out reporters for maligning teachers, their unions, and their precious summer vacation, Steven embodies the gadfly in spirit and prose.

At a conference I presented at recently, Deborah Meier noted that the language of education activists often took on a Trumponian "make public schools great again" tone, and she cautioned us to remember that for some people public education was never great. Before No Child Left Behind and a Nation at Risk, black and brown children attended under-funded schools with limited resources. To imply that public schools were progressive and democratic before corporations got involved is to disregard the lived experiences of people who have fought to make public education be the great equal-izer they never received. To insist that the constitution of each state is the roadmap for what public education should be for all students is to ignore the fact that when the constitution was written, it was never intended to represent people of color and their children. A country that denied the right to an education to generations of black people cannot expect that same system of education to close the opportunity gap it created.

As I reflect on Deb's words, I am more committed to ensuring that the education activists I work with do not commit the fatal flaw of ignoring racism and white supremacy. The battle ahead will be long and difficult, and we have no chance of winning if we fail to recognize what lies at the heart of the beast. Railing against competency-based education, personalized learning, social impact bonds, and attacks on unions is pointless unless you are willing to acknowledge how white supremacy and racism make all of these possible. If you are confused about how to begin this process, you are in luck. Steven does that for you by first addressing race and prejudice before moving on to school choice, testing, and teaching. His book is a roadmap for understanding how school reform is fueled by racism, and is a valuable tool for activists who want to win the fight.

Denisha Jones, PhD.
Assistant Professor of Education and Chair of the Education Program, Trinity Washington University

ACKNOWLEDGEMENTS

This book – and this author - would not exist without the help of so many incredible people. From the bottom of my heart, I would like to thank my second family at the Badass Teachers Association – Marla Kilfoyle, Priscilla Sanstead, Melissa Tomlinson, Denisha Jones, Gus Morales, Sue Goncarovs, Michael Flanagan, Nancy Osborne, Wilma De Soto, Larry Profitt, Jesse Turner, Terry Kalb, Owen Jackman, Sergio Flores, Kathie Wing Larson, Jamy Brice Hyde, Becca Ritchie, Tina Andres, Roberta Reid, Lee Ann Pepper Nolan, Kathleen Hagans Jesky, Michelle Murphy Ramey, Lori Gumanow and EJ Savage Kelly. I'd also like to recognize my compatriots at United Opt Out National – Ruth Rodriguez, Ceresta Smith, Zachary Rodriguez, and Erika Strauss Chavarria. Also thanks to Yohuru Williams, Rick Smith, Dick Price, Sharon Kyle, Kevin Mahoney, and of course Denny Taylor, Benjamin Taylor and David Taylor at Garn Press.

I owe a huge debt to the education blogging community especially Diane Ravitch, Anthony Cody, Russ Walsh, Julian Vasquez Heilig, Jessie Ramey, Jonathan Pelto, Mark Naison, Peter Greene, Mercedes Schneider, Jennifer Berkshire and

Emily Talmage.

Like any educator, I'm only as good as my fellow teachers. Here's a heartfelt shout out to my district colleagues Mark Fallon, Heather Clark, Denise Williams, Melissa Walters, Bethany Fenyus, Marguerite Luvara, Terrie Hoffman, Traci Churilla, Mary Cay Milliner, Michael Hofbauer, Larry McKern, Kevin Walsh, Shawn McCallister and Jill Fleming Salopek.

None of this would be possible without the essential thoughtfulness of my friends and family. You put up with me (sometimes on a daily basis) and deserve a medal. Particular thanks to Elisha Singer, Desdemona Singer, Robert Singer, Linda Singer, Jeffrey Singer, William Witt, Barbara Witt, Charlotte Perl, Larry Perl, Lora Rigatti, Adam Perl, Aaron Ankers, Michael Tutera, and Ryan Tutera.

If I've forgotten someone – and I probably have – you have my sincerest apologies.

And last but far from least, I'd like to thank YOU for reading this book. When I started my blog in July of 2014, I had no idea it would grow into the text in your hands. Beyond that first entry, I couldn't have written another word without the sustained interest of the thousands of people who log on every week to read my latest ramblings. More than anyone else, thank you.

INTRODUCTION

THE ONGOING RESISTANCE TO TRUMP, NEOLIBERALS & ANYONE ELSE TRYING TO DESTROY OUR SCHOOLS

"Most of the important things in the world have been accomplished by people who have kept on trying when there seemed to be no help at all."
Dale Carnegie

"It always seems impossible until it's done."
Nelson Mandela

Buck up, People.

I see that hopeless look on your faces. I see it because it's the same look reflected back at me in the mirror every morning.

Donald Trump is President of the United States, and he's filled his cabinet with people who are determined to destroy

15

the very offices where he's putting them in charge.

His Education Secretary doesn't believe in public schools. His Labor Secretary doesn't believe in worker's rights. His Housing chief doesn't believe in public housing. His head of Environmental Protection doesn't believe in protecting the environment. Heck! You pick a department and he's found someone to lead it who doesn't believe in doing that job!

And to top it all off, he used to have a literal white supremacist as his chief strategist.

But you know what? I'm not scared.

You know why? Because I'm still here.

Seriously.

The forces of greed and ignorance have been salivating all over the prospect of destroying public education for decades, and they haven't been able to do it.

We're still here. In almost every municipality, district or borough, our public schools remain open.

Sure, they're a bit worse for wear in some neighborhoods. But despite billions of dollars being spent to crush them under foot, we survive to fight another day.

And that day is today.

Why should we despair when we behold the glass menagerie of fools Trump has assembled to populate his administration? Glass breaks.

Why should we despair when hearing the tired rhetoric of Nazi Germany and the Jim Crow South coming out of his mouth? We defeated both! We can do so again.

Take Betsy DeVos, Trump's Education Secretary. She's a religious fanatic who's dedicated her life to destroying public schools.

I'm not scared of her. We just fought off Arne Duncan and John King – two of the Democrats' Ivy League privateers who actually knew what they were doing! If we can stop those jackholes from giving away community schools to rich corporations, we can take this rich Republican lady who never held down a real job and only knows how to get her way by bribing people to do her bidding.

Sorry, Miss Betsy, but your school vouchers aren't driving my family out of our neighborhood school so my kid can be taken advantage of by multinational corporations and Christian cults masquerading as authentic educational institutions. We're wise to your BS "School Choice" fantasies.

Then there's Rex Tillerson, another corporate vampire who'd like to suck our classrooms dry. The Exxon CEO and Trump's pick for Secretary of State is a climate denying gasoline peddler who's dimwitted enough to think he knows everything. Drawing on his zero years of experience with childhood psychology or education, he actually said aloud that struggling students were "defective products" as if they were irregular widgets being pressed out on the assembly line and unfit for service at his service stations.

I'm not worried about that gashole. He'll be too busy enriching himself in backroom deals with foreign leaders to pay much attention to our schools. He's no threat.

Okay. I'll admit the President's ex-advisor Steve Bannon made my skin crawl. Trump used to have a literal neo-Nazi propagandist as chief strategist, an alleged wife beater who apparently thinks black people don't necessarily deserve the right to vote. Well, thankfully Bannon goose-stepped his way back to Breitbart – if only he'd taken his orange-faced Reality TV star Commander-in-Chief with him.

Look, Trump is a monster and he's assembled a cabinet of

monstrosities to back him up. But that doesn't make him scary. The best way to fight monsters is to turn on the light. And we have the brightest light of all – the light of knowledge, experience, and wisdom.

We've been doing it for the past 8 years with the Democrats, people who were supposed to be our friends and allies. You think it'll be harder with GOP nitwits openly declaring themselves our enemies!?

For all the cosmetic ways President Barack Obama's administration was better, they were almost as enthusiastic about boosting privatization and making sure every child had a standardized test that was written above their level and biased towards rich white kids. All their talk about championing civil rights didn't stop them from closing poor black kids' schools and forcing them into unaccountable charter operations that often provided fewer services, achieved dismal academic results, and boosted racial segregation. All their talk about equity didn't result in any more funding for minority children – only more Common Core, unqualified Teach for America temps and testing, testing, testing. Yet their donors in the standardized testing, publishing and privatization industry raked in obscene profits.

I'm sorry if this hurts some people's rosy-eyed view of politics, but Obama was no friend to education. Plutocracy isn't just a practice on the other side of the aisle. The Democrats are almost as beholden to their corporate masters, and like good servants, they do what their rich donors tell them to do.

This isn't news to us. We've been on the outs before. In fact, we've never been on the ins.

Donald Trump? Shit! We lived through an administration that wanted to destroy us and actually knew how to do it! We can take Tiny Hands, the Bankruptcy King any day! This is a guy who couldn't make a profit running casinos – a business where the house always wins! You expect us to cower in fear that he's going to take away our schools. Son, we've fought better than you!

We just need to stop, take a deep breath and re-energize ourselves.

We need a moment of rededication, time to size up our newest antagonists, and prepare for the battles ahead.

Yes, we're surrounded on all sides. But it's never been any different.

Yes, we don't have any political party that supports us. So we'll either take over the Democrats or build our own legislative network.

I don't mean to minimize the threat. Trump represents a clear and present danger to our nation, our people and our schools. But we represent a clear and present danger to him. Even before the day he was sworn in, the clock was already ticking. He'll be lucky to last four years in the ring with us.

So in that spirit, I offer the following advice. And not just to the nation's parents, students and teachers. Nor am I speaking only to our civil rights activists, humanists and empathists. I'm not even speaking just to you, my brothers and sisters in education activism. I'm also speaking to that broken down father, teacher and activist in myself, too.

Chin up, Bucko. We aren't done yet. Not even close.

Together we can win this fight. We've been doing just that for years.

We have nothing to fear from Trump. He and the neoliberals have much to fear from us.

"Fate whispers to the warrior 'You cannot withstand the storm.' The warrior whispers back 'I am the storm.' "

Unknown

"If you want to make a permanent change, stop focusing on the size of your problems and start focusing on the size of you!"

T. Harv Eker

PART I

RACISM AND PREJUDICE

I AM RACIST AND (IF YOU'RE WHITE) YOU PROBABLY ARE, TOO

I am a white man.

I am racist.

But that's kind of redundant.

It's like saying, "I am a fish, and I am soaking wet."

In some ways, I can't help it. I don't even notice it. I live my life immersed in a world of white privilege that most of the time I frankly can't even see.

That doesn't excuse me. It doesn't mean I should just shrug and say, "What are you gonna do?"

But it does mean that the first step in removing that racism – in undoing the systematic subjugation of people of color – is recognizing my own culpability in that system.

It's like being an alcoholic. The first step is admitting the truth.

I know I've probably pissed off a lot of people with what I've just written, but this isn't about gaining new friends. And I'm sure my opinion here in this book will earn me a share of death threats, just as the original publishing of this article earned me a host of them on-line.

The initial reaction white people usually have to being called racist is – Who? Me? I can't be racist! I have a black friend! I dated a black girl once! I listen to rap music!

Or a whole host of other excuses.

First of all, relax. I don't know you. For all I know you're that one white person out there who has somehow escaped the pervasive societal attitudes that the rest of us unknowingly took in with our baby formula.

But chances are – yeah, you're a racist, too.

Second of all, I'm not talking to people of color. None of you are racist.[1]

Congratulations!

You might be a hate-filled bigoted, misogynistic, xenophobic, homophobic, prejudiced asshole.

Again, I don't know you. But *racist*? No. You can't really be that.

Here's why. Racism doesn't mean hating someone because of their race. That's a kind of prejudice.[2] And anyone can be prejudiced.

Racism is hate plus power.[3] If a black person says, "I hate white people," he is prejudiced. However, there is no system that then backs up his hatred. The police don't arrest white people more than black people for the same crimes. The judicial system doesn't give harsher sentences to white people than it does black people for the same crimes. Public schools serving a majority of white students aren't chronically underfunded. It isn't harder to get a loan or a job if you have a white-sounding name. If it did, THAT would be racism!

Get it?

So I'm sorry, white people. This means there is no such thing as reverse racism. Despite what you may see on Fox News, the only racists in America have white skin.

Don't get me wrong. There are degrees of racism. If you have a Confederate flag prominently displayed in your home in front of your personally autographed picture with David Duke, well you're probably a bit more racist than most Caucasians. But no matter what, if you're white, you've probably benefited from white supremacy and are to some degree a de facto racist.

Maybe your folks gave you a middle class upbringing in a quiet suburb. Maybe you went to a well-funded public school in a wealthy neighborhood. Maybe your dad was convicted of white collar crime and got little to no jail time. Heck! Maybe you just walked down the street once and the police didn't follow you through a convenience store or reached for their guns.

If your upbringing was in any way favored due to wealth amassed over a few generations, you benefited from white privilege. If the judicial system let you or a loved one go with a lighter sentence, you benefited. If you were not harassed by law enforcement because of your complexion, you benefited. And when you benefit from a system, you're part of it.

For every white person in America, it is almost certain that something like this happened to you at some point in your life. And you probably had no idea it was even occurring.

Good fortune becomes a self-fulfilling prophecy. People start to think they deserve it. And maybe they do, maybe they don't. But people of color who don't have such privileges certainly don't deserve their inequitable treatment.

When we fail to acknowledge that white supremacy exists or that it benefits us, white folks, we're just perpetuating that same system.

Some of you will say I'm putting too much emphasis on race. We're all the same under the skin. We shouldn't bring up the topic of racism. It just makes things worse.

Easy for you to say! You're on top of the social food chain! If we don't talk about the inherent inequalities entrenched in the system, nothing will change. Us, white folks, will continue to benefit, and black folks will continue to get the short end of the stick.

One of the biggest obstacles to solving racism is its invisibility – to white folks.

We're shielded from it because its negative effects don't reach us, and its positive effects to us are either shrugged off or we assume we deserve them.

Being racist rarely involves overt action anymore. It's become covert,[4] an entrenched sickness in all our social systems. And the only way to cure it is to make it visible – to recognize, isolate and destroy it.

I know. Some of you will say you had it tough, too. And you probably did. Few people live charmed lives. There are poor white folks. There are white people who are discriminated against because of their gender, nationality, sexual preference and/or religion.[5] But this doesn't mean you didn't benefit. There is a crossroads of American prejudice, and racism is only one of many intersecting avenues.

Maybe you were the victim sometimes, but you were probably the victor at other times, and you never even saw it coming.

The point isn't to say which malady is worse. They're all bad and all deserving of a cure. But if you really don't want to be a racist, you have to look it straight in the eye and call it by its rightful name.

You probably didn't ask to be treated differently. Most of us just want fairness. But to be on that side we have to proclaim our allegiance. We have to take a stand.

Whenever you see injustice against people of color, you must call it out. You must make yourself a part of the solution and not the problem. You must be a voice demanding the citadel of white privilege be burned to the ground.

It's not easy. You'll be called all sorts of names – bleeding heart, libtard, self-hating white, maybe even cracka – because even people of color may not understand what you're trying to do. After so many years of racial oppression by people like us with melanin deficiency, some black folks may not trust an open hand when they've been so used to expecting a fist.

But that's okay. It's understandable. The only thing to do is press on. Understanding will come – eventually.

Racism is a problem for black folks, but the solution is mostly in the hands of white people. We're the ones doing – or allowing – racism. It's our job to fix it.

And much of that work will not be in the public sphere. It will be in our own hearts.

Many of us have been socialized to be afraid of black folks. We get this from the news, movies, television, the Internet, often even our own relatives and friends. We're constantly told how dangerous black people are, how untrustworthy, how violent. But the facts don't bear this out. Given the degree of aggression – both overt and covert – black people have endured from white people over time, they have been incredibly nonviolent.[6] It is us, white people, who have been violent and inhuman. That is the legacy we hide under our fear of dark skin. We're really afraid that one day our black brothers and sisters will have had enough and give back to us all the accumulated hate of centuries.

No. We aren't responsible for slavery or Jim Crow or lynchings or a host of other horrible things. But we still benefit from them.

So it is up to us to even the scales, to treat black folks fairly and equitably with a loving heart.

That is why I make this confession. That is why I write this, even though I know that it will probably be roundly criticized or maybe just ignored.

That's why I admit I'm to some degree a racist.

It's the only way to stop being one.

WHITENESS - THE LIE MADE TRUE

"The discovery of a personal whiteness among the world's peoples is a very modern thing – a nineteenth and twentieth century matter, indeed."

W. E. B. Du Bois.[7]

What color is your skin?

You don't have to look. You know. It's a bedrock fact of your existence like your name, religion or nationality.

But go ahead and take a look. Hold out your hand and take a good, long stare.

What do you see?

White? Black? Brown?

More than likely, you don't see any of those colors.

You see some gradation, a hue somewhere in the middle, but in the back of your mind you label it black, white, brown, etc.

When I look, I see light peach with splotches of pink. But I know that I'm white, White, **WHITE**.

So where did this idea come from? If my skin isn't actually white – it's not the same white I'd find in a tube of paint, or on a piece of paper – why am I labeled white?

The answer isn't scientific, cultural or economic.

It's legal.

Yes, here in America we have a legal definition of whiteness.

It developed over time, but the earliest mention in our laws comes from the Naturalization Act of 1790.

Only 14 years after our Declaration of Independence proclaimed all people were created equal, we passed this law to define who exactly has the right to call him-or-herself an American citizen. It restricted citizenship to persons who had resided in the United States for two years, who could establish their good character in court, and who were "white" – whatever that meant.

In 1896 this idea gained even more traction in the infamous U.S. Supreme Court decision Plessy v Ferguson. The case is known for setting the legal precedent justifying segregation because it was "separate but equal." However, the particulars of the case revolve around the definition of whiteness.

Homer Plessy was kicked off the white section of a train car, and he sued – not because he thought there was anything wrong with segregation, but because he claimed he was actually white. The U.S. Supreme Court was asked to define what that means.

Notably the court took this charge very seriously, admitting how important it is to be able to distinguish between white and non-white. Justices claimed whiteness as a kind of property – very valuable property – the denial of which could incur legal sanction.

In its decision, the court said:[8]

> If he be a white man and assigned to a colored coach, he may have his action for damages from the company for being deprived of his so-called property. Upon the other hand, if he be a colored man and be so assigned, he has been deprived of no property, since he is not lawfully entitled to the reputation of being a white man.

Plessy wasn't the only one to seek legal action over this. Native Americans were going to court claiming that they, too, were white and should be treated as such. Much has been written about the struggle of various ethnic groups – Irish, Slovak, Polish, etc. – to be accepted under this term. No matter how you define it, most groups wanted it to include them and theirs.

However, it wasn't until 1921 when a strong definition of white was written in the "Emergency Quota and Immigration Acts." It states:[9]

> "White person" has been held to include an Armenian born in Asiatic Turkey, a person of but one-sixteenth Indian blood, and a Syrian, but not to include Afghans, American Indians, Chinese, Filipinos, Hawaiians, Hindus, Japanese, Koreans, negroes; nor does white person include a person having one fourth of African blood, a person in whom Malay blood predominates, a person whose father was a German and whose mother was a Japanese, a person whose father was a white Canadian and whose mother was an Indian woman, or a person whose mother was a Chinese and whose father was the son of a Portuguese father and a Chinese mother.

So there you have it – whiteness – legally defined and enforceable as a property value.

It's not a character trait. It's certainly not a product of the color wheel. It's a legal definition, something we made up. **THIS** is the norm. **THAT** is not.

Admitting that leads to the temptation to disregard whiteness, to deny its hold on society. But doing so would be to ignore an important facet of the social order. As Brian Jones writes, the artificiality of whiteness doesn't make it any less real:[10]

It's very real. It's real in the same way that Wednesday is real. But it's also made up in the same way that Wednesday is made up.

You couldn't go around saying, "I don't believe in Wednesdays." You wouldn't be able to function in society. You could try to change the name, you could try to change the way we conceptualize the week, but you couldn't ignore the way it is now.

And whiteness is still a prominent feature of America's social structure.

Think about it. A range of skin colors have become the dominant identifier here in America. We don't like to talk about it, but the shade of your epidermis still means an awful lot.

It often determines the ease with which you can get a good job, a bank loan or buy a house in a prosperous neighborhood. It determines the ease with which you can go to a well-resourced school, a district democratically controlled by the community and your access to advanced placement classes. And it determines the degree of safety you have when being confronted by the police.

But to have whiteness as a signifier of the good, the privileged, we must imply an opposite. It's not a term disassociated from others. Whiteness implies blackness.

It's no accident. Just as the concept of whiteness was invented to give certain people an advantage, the concept of blackness was invented to subjugate others. However, this idea goes back a bit further. We had a delineated idea of blackness long before we legalized its opposite.

The concept of blackness began in the Virginia colonies in the 1600s. European settlers were looking to get rich quick through growing tobacco. But that's a labor-intensive process and before mechanization it frankly cost too much in salaries for landowners to make enough of a profit to ensure great wealth. Moreover, settlers weren't looking to grow a modest amount of tobacco for use only in the colonies. They wanted to produce enough to supply the global market. That required mass production and a disregard for humanity.

So tobacco planters decided to reduce labor costs through slavery. They tried enslaving the indigenous population, but Native Americans knew the land too well and would escape quicker than they could be replaced.

Planters also tried using indentured servants – people who defaulted on their debts and had to sell themselves into slavery for a limited time. However, this caused a lot of bad feeling in communities. When husbands, sons and relatives were forced into servitude while their friends and neighbors remained free, bosses faced social and economic recriminations from the general population. Moreover, when an indentured servant's time was up, if he could raise the capital, he now had all the knowledge and experience to start his own tobacco plantation and compete with his former boss.

No. Planters needed a more permanent solution. That's where the idea came from to kidnap Africans and bring them to Virginia as slaves. This was generational servitude, no time limits, no competition, low cost.

It's important to note that it took time for this kind of slavery to take root in the colonies. Part of this is due to various ideas about the nature of Africans. People at the time didn't all have our modern prejudices. Also it took time for the price of importing human beings from another continent to become less than that of buying indentured servants.

The turning point was Bacon's Rebellion in 1676. Hundreds of slaves and indentured servants came together and deposed the governor of Virginia, burned down plantations and defended themselves against planter militias for months afterwards. The significance of this event was not lost on the landowners of the time. What we now call "white" people and "black" people had banded together against the landowners. If things like this were to become more frequent, the tobacco industry would be ruined, or at very least much less profitable for the planters.

After the rebellion was put down, the landed gentry had to find a way to stop such large groups of people from ever joining together in common cause again. The answer was the racial caste system we still experience today.

The exact meaning of "white" and "black" – or "colored" – was mostly implied, but each group's social mobility was rigidly defined for the first time. Laws were put in place to categorize people and provide benefits for some and deprivations for others. So white people were then allowed to own property, own guns, participate in juries, serve on militias, and do all kinds of things that were to be forever off-limits to black people. It's important to understand that black people were not systematically barred from these things before.

Just imagine how effective this arrangement was. It gave white people a permanent, unearned social position above black people. No matter how hard things could get for impoverished whites, they could never sink below this level. They would always enjoy these privileges, and by extension enjoy the deprivation of blacks as proof of their own white superiority. Not only did it stop whites from joining together with blacks in common cause, it gave whites a reason to support the *status quo*. Sound familiar? It should.

However, for black people the arrangement was devastating.

As Brian Jones puts it:[10]

For the first time in human history, the color of one's skin had a political significance. It never had a political significance before. Now there was a reason to assign a political significance to dark skin – it's an ingenious way to brand someone as a slave. It's a brand that they can never wash off, that they can never erase, that they can never run away from. There's no way out. That's the ingeniousness of using skin color as a mark of degradation, as a mark of slavery.

All that based on pigmentation.

Our political and social institutions have made this difference in appearance paramount in the social structure, but what causes it? What is the essential difference between white people and black people, and can it in any way justify these social distinctions, privileges and deprivations?

Science tells us why human skin comes in different shades. It's based on the amount of melanin we possess, a pigment that not only gives color but blocks the body from absorbing harmful ultraviolet radiation from the sun. Everyone has some melanin. Fair skinned people can even temporarily increase the amount they have by additional solar exposure – tanning.

If the body absorbs too much UV radiation, it can cause

cancers or produce birth defects in the next generation. That's why groups of people who historically lived closer to the equator possess more melanin than those further from it. This provided an evolutionary advantage.

However, the human body needs vitamin D, which often comes from sunlight. Having a greater degree of melanin can stop the body from absorbing the necessary Vitamin D and – if another source isn't found - health problems like Sickle-cell anemia can occur.

That's why people living further from the equator developed lighter skin over time. Humanity originated in Africa, but as peoples migrated north they didn't need the extra melanin since they received less direct sunlight. Likewise, they benefited from less melanin and therefore easier absorption of Vitamin D from the sunlight they did receive.

That's the major difference between people of different colors.

Contrary to the persistent beliefs of many Americans, skin color doesn't determine work ethic, intelligence, honesty, strength, or any other character trait.

In the 19th through the 20th Centuries, we created a whole field of science called eugenics to prove otherwise. We tried to show that each race had dominant traits and some races were better than others.

However, modern science has disproven every scrap of it. Eugenics is now considered a pseudoscience. Everywhere in public we loudly proclaim that judgments like these based on race are unacceptable. Yet the pattern of positive consequences for light skinned people and negative consequences for dark skinned people persists. And few of us want to identify, discuss or – God forbid – confront it.

And that's where we are today.

We in America live in a society that still subscribes to the essentially nonsensical definitions of the past. Both white and black people have been kept in their place because of them.

In each socio-economic bracket people have common cause that goes beyond skin color. But the ruling class has used a racial caste system to stop us from joining together against them.

This is obvious to most black people because they deal with the negative consequences of it every day. White people, however, are constantly bombarded by tiny benefits without noticing they're present at all. White people take it as their due – this is what all people deserve. And, yes, it IS what all people deserve, but it is not what all people are receiving!

We are faced with a difficult task. We must somehow both understand that our ideas about race are socially constructed while taking arms against them. We must accept that whiteness and blackness are bogus terms and yet they dramatically affect our lives. We must preserve all that makes us who we are while fighting for the common humanity of all.

And we can't do that by simply ignoring skin color. That kind of colorblindness only helps perpetuate the *status quo*. Instead, we must pay attention to inequalities based on the racial divide and actively work to counteract them.

Perhaps another way of looking at it would be to insist that there are no white people and black people. There are only racists and anti-racists.

Which will you be?

PREJUDICE OF POVERTY - WHY AMERICANS HATE THE POOR AND WORSHIP THE RICH

Take a breath.

Take a deep breath. Let your lungs expand. Let the air collect inside you.

Hold it.

Now exhale slowly. Feels good doesn't it? You'd never realize there are hundreds of contaminants floating invisibly in that air. Dirt, germs, pollution – all entering your body unnoticed but stopped by your immune system.

If only we had such a natural defense against prejudice. Racism, classism, xenophobia, sexism, homophobia – we take all that in with every breath, too.

It may not seem like it, but all these value judgments are inherent in American culture. They're as much a part of life in the United States as the flag, football and apple pie. And to a greater or lesser extent, you have subconsciously accepted them to help construct your ideas of normality.

What does it mean to be a man? What does it mean to be a woman? How should black people be treated? To whom is it appropriate to be sexually attracted? What makes a person poor and why? All of these questions and so many more have been answered one way or another for us by the dominant culture. Not everyone accepts this perceived wisdom, but most of us have swallowed these solutions whole without thought, logic or criticism – and we don't even know it's happened.

Take our preconceptions about wealth and poverty.

Well-paying jobs are drying up. Minimum wage work is becoming more common. Salaries are shrinking while productivity is increasing. Meanwhile the cost of living continues to rise as does the cost of getting an education.

Yet we still cling to the belief that all rich people deserve their wealth and all poor people deserve their poverty.

When we hear about someone on Welfare or food stamps, we sneer. The average conception is that this person is probably faking it. He or she could have earned enough to avoid public assistance, but he or she isn't trying hard enough.

Moreover, we **KNOW** with a certainty that goes beyond mere empiricism that many of the poor still manage to buy the newest sneakers, have flat screen TVs, and eat nothing but porterhouse steaks.

You can hear this kind of story uttered with perfect certainty from the mouths of white, middle class people everywhere. They don't mind helping people who are really in need, they say, but most poor folks are gaming the system.

Never once do they stop to consider that this story about impoverished individuals living better than middle class Americans is itself one of the most pervasive myths in our society. We know it the same way we know all Polish people are dumb, all Asians are smart and all Black people love fried chicken and watermelon. However, none of this "knowledge" is supported by the facts. Look at the Supplemental Nutrition Assistance Program (SNAP). According to the New York Times:[11]

> Allegations of fraud, including an informal economy in which food stamps are turned into cash or used to buy liquor, gasoline or other items besides food have been used to argue that the program is out of control. In fact, the black market accounts for just over 1 percent of the total food stamp program, which is far less than fraud in other government programs like Medicare and Medicaid.

If you include erroneous payments because of mistakes on applications, overall loss to the food stamp program comes to 4%, according to the Department of Agriculture. Compare that to the 10% lost to Medicare and Medicaid – programs no one is calling to be cut or eliminated.

But figures like these don't convince the average American. We're so certain that all or most poor people are just lazy parasites. Everyone "knows" some low-income person they deem to be living too high for their circumstances.

And, yes, sometimes you do see an impoverished individual not wearing rags. Sometimes you do peek into an indigent person's hovel and see a pair of new shoes, an electronic device, or a game system.

How does this happen?

Debt.

Credit card companies are waiting in the shadows to extend a line of credit to just about anybody. It's a safe bet for these businesses. If they give you money today, they can charge exorbitant rates of interest – even more so with the highest risk clientele. But there isn't much risk when almost anyone can take a job as a state constable or bail recovery agent to hunt down debtors and bring them to economic justice.

If you see a destitute child with new sneakers, his parents probably bought them with plastic. If you see an X-Box in a needy person's house, chances are that wasn't paid for in cash. They used the charge plate and will end up paying for that game system many times its worth.

It's a strategy not limited to the poor. Even middle class folks are drowning up to their eyeballs in debt. As wages have decreased, people living above the poverty line have used their credit cards to keep a middle class standard of living. But they're paying for it with huge portions of their paychecks going to these credit card companies.

Is it any wonder then that some of the poor intermittently try to preserve the illusion for their kids even if it forces them into back payments they can less afford than the rest of us? Yet we take a simple satisfaction looking down on them for trying to mitigate their circumstances the same way we do.

It's an obvious truth we refuse to see. *You're poor? You don't look poor enough. How dare you survive on anything other than a crust of bread!* On the one hand we demand the poor pull themselves up by their own bootstraps, but when they take advantage of even a flawed system, we blame them for doing so and dub them social parasites. Moreover, we never stop to consider that crippling debt with high interest can never pull someone out of poverty. It can only occasionally soften the edges.

But even that infuriates some of us! We begrudge the poor food, comfort, anything and everything! Those are my tax dollars and they're not going to pay for anyone's free ride, we say. (Even if we didn't pay for it, it's an awfully short ride, and it isn't free.)

Our money won't be wasted on something as useless as humanitarian aid. Regrettably, we don't stop to consider how little of our taxes are actually going to help the less fortunate.

Let's say you make $50,000 a year. That means you pay $36 toward food stamps.[12] That's ten cents a day – the same amount many charities ask to help feed starving children in Africa.

If you add all safety net programs, the cost only goes up an additional $6 a year. That doesn't seem like a huge chunk of my taxes. Honestly, do you begrudge needy people less than the price of a meal for a family of four at Bennigan's?

By and large, your tax bill isn't going to the poverty-stricken. It's going to wealthy corporations. Over the course of a year, you pay $6,000[13] for various forms of corporate welfare.

You read that right. Six K. Six grand. Six thou. Those are your tax dollars at work, too. And it's a much larger burden on your bank account than the $42 you shell out for the poor.

What do you get for that $6,000 outlay? It includes at least $870 to direct subsidies and grants for corporations. An additional $870 goes to offset corporate taxes. Another $1,231 goes to plug holes in the federal budget from revenue lost to corporate tax havens. Oh! And don't forget a sizable chunk for subsidies to Big Oil companies that are polluting our skies and fueling climate change and global warming.

Most of your money isn't going to feed hungry children. It's going to recoup losses for giant transnational corporations like Apple and GE that hide their money overseas to boost profits and avoid paying taxes for things we all need like schools, police, and fire departments.

This money subsidizes giant multi-national corporations that are already making billions and billions of dollars in profit each year. In the past decade alone, corporations have doubled their profits – all while reducing their American workforces and sending jobs overseas. Yet we only complain about poor folks using food stamps and buying new sneakers on credit.

Why is that? Why does it only bother us when poor people get help and not when huge corporations do?

Part of it is the media. We've been convinced that big business deserves its money and poor people don't. Another part of it is that these facts often go underreported. Movies and TV shows love portraying the parasite poor person but rarely portray the corporate leech. Outside of "It's a Wonderful Life" and "A Christmas Carol," the wealthy are usually portrayed in the most positive light possible and not as addicts hoarding cash they don't need to compete with each other in a childish game of one-upmanship.

Finally, there is the racial and sexual element. By and large, corporations are run by white males. The poor are mostly black, brown and though women make up a slightly higher percentage than men, it is often conceptualized as uniquely female. Take the term Welfare Queen. Why is there no Welfare King? How telling that our conception only allows for one gender in this role!

The reality is much different. The true Welfare Queens are Big Businesses. They make unprecedented profits and avoid paying taxes on them. They have tons of cash on hand but never can seem to get enough. And if we increased the corporate tax rate to what it was in the 1950s when the United States was more prosperous than it has ever been, these same corporations would still be Filthy. Stinking. Rich.

So the next time you hear someone blaming the poor for

gobbling up your taxes, remember the facts. First, it's simply not true. There is no widespread fraud by the poor. They are not gaming the system. They are not putting an undue burden on the middle class. However, big business **IS** in fact cheating you out of income. Business people are getting fabulously wealthy on your dime – and even if we stopped subsidizing them, they'd still be fabulously wealthy!

Finally, don't ignore the racial component. Would middle class Caucasians still complain so vehemently about the poor if they weren't mostly talking about Black people, Latinos and women? I doubt it.

We may breathe in these prejudices but we're not helpless. It's up to all of us to dispel these myths, not to let them stand, to confront them every time they come up. And, yes, I mean **EVERY. TIME.**

The only immune system we have as a society is education, knowledge, wisdom. And once you know the truth, don't let anyone get away with this kind of racist, classist bullshit.

DECOLONIZING THROUGH DIALOGUE - AUTHENTIC TEACHING IN THE AGE OF TESTING AND COMMON CORE

If you're not careful, being a public school teacher can become an act of colonization.

This is especially true if you're a white teacher like me with classes of mostly black students. But it's not the only case. As an educator, no matter who you are or whom you teach, you're a symbol of authority and you get that power from the dominant structures in our society.

Believe it or not, our schools are social institutions, so one of their chief functions is to help recreate the social order. Students enter as malleable lumps of clay and exit mainly in the shapes we decide upon. Therefore, as an educator, it's hard not to fall into the habit of molding young minds into the shapes society has decided are appropriate.

In some ways this is inevitable. In others, it's even desirable. But it also runs against the best potential of education.

In short, this isn't what a teacher should be. My job in front of the classroom isn't to make my students into anything. It's to give them the opportunity to generate the spark that turns them into their best selves. And the people who ultimately should be the most empowered in this process are the students themselves.

But it's easier said than done.

The danger is best expressed in that essential book for any teacher, *Pedagogy of the Oppressed*,[14] where Paulo Freire writes:

> Worse yet, it turns them – the students – into 'containers,' into 'receptacles' to be filled by the teacher. The more completely she fills the receptacles, the better a teacher she is. The more meekly the receptacles permit themselves to be filled, the better students they are.

In most cases this means Eurocentrism – a kind of worship of all things white and denigration of all things black, brown and all pigments between.

We take the status quo and find every blind justification for it. In fact, this can become the curriculum itself. Every counter-narrative, every criticism of the power structure then naturally becomes a danger. Revisionist history becomes history. European philosophy becomes the only accepted definition of rationality. Ideologies of empire become obvious and inescapable. White becomes the norm and racism, misogyny, homophobia, xenophobia all become hidden and internalized.

You've heard the criticism of curriculums focusing exclusively on dead white males. This is why.

And not only does it silence minority voices, it reinforces a false view of the world. Folk singer Tom Paxton made that clear in this classic song:

"What Did You Learn In School Today?"[15]

What did you learn in school today,
Dear little boy of mine?
What did you learn in school today,
Dear little boy of mine?

I learned that Washington never told a lie,
I learned that soldiers seldom die,
I learned that everybody's free,
And that's what the teacher said to me,
And that's what I learned in school today,
That's what I learned in school.

What did you learn in school today,
Dear little boy of mine?
What did you learn in school today,
Dear little boy of mine?

I learned the policemen are my friends,
I learned that justice never ends,
I learned that murderers pay for their crimes,
Even if we make a mistake sometimes,
And that's what I learned in school today,
That's what I learned in school

What did you learn in school today,
Dear little boy of mine?
What did you learn in school today,
Dear little boy of mine?

I learned that war is not so bad,
I learned about the great ones we've had.
We fought in Germany and in France
And some day I might get my chance.
And that's what I learned in school today,
That's what I learned in school

What did you learn in school today,
Dear little boy of mine?
What did you learn in school today,
Dear little boy of mine?

I learned our government must be strong,
It's always right and never wrong!
Our leaders are the finest men
And we elect them again and again,
And that's what I learned in school today,
That's what I learned in school

We can see why this kind of teaching is valued. It reinforces the status quo. But at its core education is essentially subversive. It supports new ways of thinking. It is by definition revolutionary. When you encourage students to think for themselves, some may come to conclusions that differ from the norm. This is entirely healthy and the only way societies can grow and change. But it's inimical to the people in power who often are in charge of the educational system. They don't want new ideas if those ideas will challenge their hold on the reins of power. After all, it wasn't because Socrates' lessons supported the Athenian elite that he was forced to drink hemlock.

So we're left with a real quandary. How do teachers remain free to inspire while being a part of a system that doesn't value inspiration?

The natural forces of society work against authentic teaching like gravity pulling at a rocket. Unless you're actively pushing against the ground, the most natural thing in the world is to just go with the flow. The textbook says this is the way. Teacher training programs often agree. Cooperating teachers who have been in the classroom for decades back it up. This is the best method. Just keep it up.

But it's not. And you shouldn't. There is another way even though it's hard to see. And **THAT'S** often what you need to be doing for your students.

Let me pause at this point to make one thing clear – I don't have all the answers.

I am no expert in how to do this. I have fallen victim to it myself more often than I'd like to admit. It may be next to impossible to avoid the accepted route much of the time. But anyone who wants to be a good teacher must at least try.

If we really want to provide the best service to our students, their parents and the community, we have to break out of the mold. We have to allow our students the chance of seeing the world their own way and not just our version of it.

The best ways I've found to do this are through careful selection of texts, use of Socratic Seminars, and allowing as much choice as possible in assignments.

When selecting texts, you want to be as inclusive as possible. Provide students with the widest possible range of authors and opinions. In Language Arts, this means purposeful multiculturalism. It means authors of color being prized equally with the European canon. It means women and transgender authors. It means authors subscribing to a wide range of beliefs and skepticisms. And it means accepting genres and forms that are often devalued like song lyrics, rap, Manga, graphic novels, and any others that can be considered deep, substantial texts.

Finding such sources can be exhausting, but it's also exhila-rating. Unfortunately, not all schools permit teachers to do this to the same degree. Some districts mandate teachers only use certain texts already approved by the school board. Others provide a list of approved texts from which teachers can pick.

Each educator will have to find ways to navigate the system. It's best if you can find support from administrators and from the community for what you want to do and go from there. But this can be a challenging road especially in our era of high stakes testing and Common Core which values authentic teaching not at all.

Another essential tool is class discussion. You may or may not be able to broaden the texts being discussed, but you can usually provide space for students to discuss those texts in class.

My 8th graders and I use the Socratic Seminar method of discussion extensively.

With almost every piece of literature, I write guided open-ended questions for the students to consider. The questions come out of the text, but I try to focus on queries that will get students thinking about how the text relates to their lives, gender, and economic issues, questions of theme, race, and opportunities to make connections of every type. Eventually, I even allow students to begin writing these questions them-selves.

The way I see it, my role is essentially an opportunity maker. It isn't about finding an answer that will please me, the teacher. It's about exploring the subject. It's not about what I think. It's about what students think. And that makes all the difference.

Finally, I've found it beneficial to allow students choice in their assignments.

There are many ways for students to demonstrate knowledge. They can write essays, take a test, create a collage, design a PowerPoint presentation, make an iMovie, act out a scene, etc. I try to expose students to multiple formats the first half of the year and then give them increased choice in how they'd like to express themselves in the second half.

Not only does this free students to think, it encourages the deepest kind of learning. It makes the lessons vital, important and intrinsic.

All of these approaches share a common feature – dialogue. They put the student, the teacher, and the author in a vital relationship. They take steps to equalize that relationship so that one isn't more important than the others. It's not just what the author, teacher or student thinks – it's the interrelationship of the three.

Ultimately, it's up to the student to decide the relative value of the results. Sure, they get grades. Sure, the system will judge students based on those grades. But the value of those grades isn't as important as the resultant learning and the value students place on the experience.

To me, that's the best kind of learning. And it's the result of authentic teaching and dialogue.

It is the most inimical thing to colonization. Students are not enslaved to a system. They aren't in servitude to a prepackaged group of ideas and norms.

They are valued and empowered.

Isn't that what we're supposed to be doing for them?

WHITE PEOPLE NEED TO STOP SNICKERING AT BLACK NAMES

As a public school teacher, few things give me as much anxiety as getting my student rosters for the first time.

I look over the list of names for my incoming children and cringe.

How do I pronounce that?

Every year it never fails – there's always at least four or five names I've never seen before – or at least never spelled quite like **THAT**!

As a white teacher in a district with a majority of black students but very few black teachers, there are not really many people to turn to for guidance.

And if I don't figure it out soon, I'll be making a pretty terrible first impression. No one likes to have their name butchered, especially children, especially if an adult is doing it, and especially if that adult is a different color than they are.

The only solution I've found is to soldier on with the first day's attendance and just try my best:

Me: Shah-NEE-Qwa?

Child: Shah-NAY-Qwa.

Me: JAY-Marcus?

Child: JAH-Marcus.

It's uncomfortable, but I get through it and eventually learn.

However, one thing I've stopped doing is going to other white people for help. That's a recipe for disaster.

It almost always turns into an exercise in subtle racism and white supremacy. No matter who the person is, no matter how kind, caring or empathetic, the reaction to unique black names is most often derision.

White people snicker and use the situation as the impetus for telling stories about other black names that they thought were even more outrageous.

It's not that we're trying to be hateful. I don't think we even recognize it as racist, but it is.

We use the situation as an opportunity for bonding. ***THOSE** people who are not like you and me – **THEY** name their children things like **THIS**! Not like you and me who name our children more respectably.*

Make no mistake. This is racist behavior. We are emphasizing the otherness of an entire group of people to put ourselves over and above them.

It's bigoted, discriminatory, prejudicial and just plain dumb.

What's wrong with black names anyway? What about them is so unacceptable?

We act as if only European and Anglicized names are reasonable. But I don't have to go far down my rosters to find white kids with names like Braelyn, Declyn, Jaydon, Jaxon, Gunner or Hunter. I've never heard white folks yucking it up over those names.

I can't imagine why white people even expect people of color to have the same sorts of names as we do. When you pick the label by which your child will be known, you often resort to a shared cultural history. *My great-great-grandfather was David, so I'll honor his memory by calling my firstborn son the same. Jennifer is a name that's been in my family for generations so I'll reconnect with that history by calling my daughter by the same name.*

Few black people in America share this same culture with white people. If a black man's great-great-grandfather's name was David, that might not be the name he was born with – it may have been chosen for him – forced upon him – by his slave master. It should be obvious why African Americans may be uncomfortable reconnecting with that history.

Many modern black names are, in fact, an attempt to reconnect with the history that was stolen from them. Names like Ashanti, Imani and Kenya have African origins. Others are religious. Names like Aaliyah, Tanisha and Aisha are traditionally Muslim. Some come from other languages – for example Monique, Chantal and Andre all come from French. I can't understand why any of that is seen as worthy of ridicule.

Still other names don't even attempt to reconnect with a lost past – they try to forge ahead and create a new future. The creativity and invention of black names is seldom recognized by White America. We pretend that creating names anew shows a lack of imagination, when in reality it shows just the opposite!

Creating something new can be as simple as taking an Anglicized name and spelling it in inventive ways. Punctuation marks also can be utilized in unusual positions to add even more distinctiveness such as in the names Mo'nique and D'Andre.

At other times, they follow a cultural pattern to signify them as uniquely African American using prefixes such as La/Le, Da/De, Ra/Re, or Ja/Je and suffixes such as -ique/iqua, -isha, and -aun/-awn.

And for the ultimate in creativity, try mixing and matching various influences and techniques. For instance, LaKeisha has elements from both French and African roots. Other names like LaTanisha, DeShawn, JaMarcus, DeAndre, and Shaniqua were created in the same way.

This is something all cultures do. They evolve to meet the needs of people in a given time and place. Yet when it comes to people of color, we white folks whoop and guffaw at it. Heck! When we can't find black names far enough out of our mainstream, we even make them up!

Don't believe me? Have you heard of La-a? The story goes that a black girl was given that name and a white person asked how it was pronounced. The black woman said her name was La-DASH-ah. This is often followed by a punchline of black vernacular.

Har! Har! Har!

But it's not even true! According to Snopes,[16] this is a made up story. It's the American version of a Polish joke and demonstrates how far white people will go to laugh at black culture.

The great comedy duo Key and Peele[17] tried to call attention to this in their outstanding substitute teacher sketches. In a series of short routines, an almost exclusively white classroom gets a black substitute teacher from the inner city schools. Mr. Garvey is expecting black names, so he pronounces the students' middle class white names as if they were African

American.

Almost everyone loves this sketch. It gets universal laughs, but wait until it's over. Too many white folks try to continue the giggles by then talking about crazy black names they've encountered. But that's not at all the point Key and Peele were trying to make! They were trying to show how cultural context shapes our expectations of proper names. Mr. Garvey is worthy of our laughter because his expectations are out-of-sync with his surroundings. When we expect all African Americans to have European or Anglicized names, we're just as out of touch as Mr. Garvey. But like Dave Chappelle's comedy, sometimes the person laughing the loudest is getting something the comedian didn't intend at all.

Maybe it wouldn't be so bad if black names just generated snickers. However, white culture actually selects against people with black sounding names.

Countless studies[18] have shown how much more difficult it is for someone with a black sounding name to get a job, a loan or an apartment than it is for someone with a white sounding name. It's one of the most obvious features of white supremacy. You may not like black names, personally, but do these people deserve to suffer for embracing their own culture?

Moreover, having a European or Anglicized name is no guarantee of fair treatment. It certainly didn't help Michael Brown or Freddie Gray.

If we're really going to treat people equitably, an easy place to begin is with black names. White people, stop the laughter and giggles. I used to do it, myself, until I thought about it. Yes, I was guilty of the same thing. But I stopped. You can, too.

It's not the biggest thing in the world. It's not even the most pressing thing. It's not a matter of guilt. It's a matter of fairness.

Because when the final roll call is taken of all America's racists and bigots, do you really want your name to be on the list?

A MOMENT OF SILENCE FOR MICHAEL BROWN

NOTE: Michael Brown died on August 9, 2014. Later that year on November 24, it was announced that Missouri police officer Darren Wilson would not be indicted in Brown's death. This article was written two days later, and it describes what took place in my classroom at that specific time. Though it resonates beyond that moment, any attempt to change its temporal setting would detract from its meaning.

Michael Brown has been dead for more than 100 days.

Yet he was in my classroom this morning.

He stared up at me from 22 sets of eyes, out of 22 faces, with 22 pairs of mostly Black and Brown childish cheeks.

The day after it was announced Missouri police Officer Darren Wilson would not be indicted in the shooting death of the unarmed Black teen my class was eerily quiet.

There was no yelling.

No singing or humming or tapping either.

No one played keep away with anyone else's pencil or laughed about something someone had said or done the night before.

No conversation about what so-and-so was wearing or arguments about the football game.

My first period class filed into the room and collapsed into their seats like they'd been up all night.

Perhaps they had been.

By the time the morning announcements ended and I had finished taking the 8th graders attendance, I had come to a decision.

I had to address it.

There was simply no way to ignore what we were all thinking and feeling. No way to ignore the ghost haunting our hearts and minds.

"May I ask you something?" I said turning to the class.

They just stared.

"Would you mind if we had a moment of silence for Michael Brown?"

I've never seen relief on so many faces all at once.

It was like I had pulled splinters from out of 22 pairs of hands with a single tug.

The White teacher was going to acknowledge Black pain. In here, they wouldn't have to hide it. They could be themselves.

Some mumbled affirmatives but most had already begun memorializing. There had been silence in their hearts since last night. Silence after the rage.

How else to deal with a reality like ours? Young men of color can be gunned down in the street and our justice system rules it isn't even worth investigating in a formal trial. The police are free to use deadly force with impunity so long as they tell a grand jury they felt threatened by their unarmed alleged assailant. And if a community can't control its anger and frustration, it's the oppressed people's fault.

These are bitter pills to swallow for adults. How much harder for the young ones just starting out?

So we bowed our heads in silence.

I've never heard a sound quite like this emptiness. Footsteps pattered in the hall, an adult's voice could be heard far away giving directions. But in our room you could almost hear your own heart beating. What a lonely sound, more like a rhythm than any particular note of the scale.

But as we stood there together it was somehow less lonely. All those solitary hearts beating with a single purpose.

I made sure to do this in all of my classes today.

The first thing I did was make this same request – "Do you mind if we have a moment of silence for Michael Brown?"

They all agreed.

In most classes this became a springboard for discussion. No grades, no lesson plans, just talk.

We talked about who Brown was and what had happened to him. We talked about the grand jury and the evidence it had considered. We talked about what their parents had told them.

And as you might expect, speaking about Brown was like a séance inviting a long line of specters into our classroom – Trayvon Martin, Eric Garner, Emmett Till, Dr. Martin Luther King, Jr. – fathers, brothers, classmates.

Some groups talked more than others. Some students spoke softly and with an eloquence beyond their years. Many only shook their heads.

One boy asked me, "Why does this keep happening, Mr. Singer?"

It was the question of which I had been most afraid. As a teacher, it's always uncomfortable to admit the limits of your knowledge. But I tried to be completely honest with him.

"I really don't know," I said, "But let's not forget that question. It's a really good one."

Every class was different. In some we spent a long time on it. In others, we moved on more quickly.

But in each one, I made sure to look into their eyes – each and every one – before the moment ended.

I didn't say it aloud, but I wanted them to know something.

We live in an uncertain world. There are people out there who will hate you just because of the color of your skin. They will hate you because of your religion or your parents or whom you love.

But in this room, I want you to know you are safe, you are cherished and you are loved.

I hope they understand.

For me this is not just an academic concern. It's personal.

I have devoted my life to these children.

Some of my colleagues say that I've gone too far. That what happened to Michael Brown and issues of racism aren't education issues, they aren't things that should concern teachers.

If not, I don't know what is.

Our society segregates public schools into Black and White.

It defunds the Black schools, closes them, and funnels the wastrels into privatized for-profit charters while leaving the best facilities and Cadillac funding for the elite and privileged.

And we allow it. Our deformed society leads to deformed citizens and a deformed parody of justice.

My room may be haunted. I teach among the ghosts of oppression. But that's the thing about phantoms. They demand their due – honesty.

It's all I have to give.

I AM A PUBLIC SCHOOL TEACHER - GIVE ME ALL THE REFUGEES YOU'VE GOT!

Come into my classroom any day of the week and you'll see refugees.

That little Iraqi boy slumped over a book written in Arabic while the rest of the class reads the same story in English. Those twin girls blinking back memories of the Bosnian War as they try to underline possessive nouns on an English worksheet. That brown-skinned boy compulsively rocking back-and-forth in his seat fighting back tears wondering when his dad is going to come home from prison.

Every day, every hour, every minute, our public schools are places of refuge for children seeking asylum – fugitives, emigres, exiles, the lost, the displaced, dear hearts seeking a kind word and a caring glance.

Some may shudder or sneer at the prospect of giving shelter

to people in need, but that is the reality in our public schools. In the lives of many, many children we provide the only stability, the only safety, the only love they get all day.

And, yes, I do mean love. I love my students. Each and every one of them. Sometimes they are far from lovable. Sometimes they look at me with distrust. They bristle at assignments. They jump when redirected. But those are the ones I try to love the most, because they are the ones most in need.

I told a friend once that I had a student who had escaped from Iraq. His parents had collaborated with the U.S. military and received death threats for their efforts. So he and his family fled to my hometown so far away from his humid desert heartland.

I told her how difficult it was trying to communicate with a student who spoke hardly any English. I complained about budget cuts that made it next to impossible to get an English Language Learner (ELL) instructor to help me more than once a week. And her response was, "Do you feel safe teaching this kid?"

Do I feel safe? The question had never occurred to me. Why wouldn't I feel safe? I don't expect ISIS to track him down across the Atlantic Ocean to my class. Nor do I expect this sweet little guy is going to do anything to me except practice his English.

In one of my first classrooms, I had a dozen refugees from Yugoslavia. They had escaped from Slobodan Milošević's ethnic cleansing. Yet you'd never know unless they told you. They were some of the most well-behaved, thoughtful, intelligent children I've had the pleasure to teach. They were always smiling, so happy to be here. They approached every assignment with a seriousness well beyond their years.

But sometimes you'd see a shadow cross their faces. Occasionally you'd hear them whispering among themselves. I was so new I didn't know any better but to come down on them. But later they told me what they had been talking about, what they had been thinking about – how our discussion of the British king Henry V's military campaign in France in the 15th century had brought back memories. They taught me that day. Every year I learn so much from my children.

My high poverty school doesn't get a lot of refugees from overseas these days. But we're overwhelmed with exiles from our own neighborhood. I can't tell you how many children I've had in class who start off the year at one house and then move to another. I can't tell you how many come to school bruised and beaten. I can't tell you how many ask a moment of my time between classes, during my planning period, or after school just to talk.

Last week one of my students walked up to me and said, "I'm having a nervous breakdown."

Class had just been dismissed. I had a desk filled to the ceiling with ungraded essays. I still had to make copies for tomorrow's parent-teacher conferences. I had gotten to none of it earlier because I had to cover another class during my planning period. But I pushed all of that aside and talked with my student for over an hour.

And I'm not alone. On those few days I get to leave close to on time, I see other teachers doing just like me conferencing and tutoring kids after school.

It was a hard conversation. I had to show him he was worth something. I had to make him feel that he was important to other people and that people cared about him. I hope I was successful. He left with a handshake and a smile.

He may not be from far away climes, but he's a refugee, too. He's seeking a safe place, a willing ear, a kind word.

So you'll forgive me if I sigh impatiently when some in the media and in the government complain about the United States accepting more refugees. What a bunch of cowards!

They act as if it's a burden. They couldn't be farther from the truth. It's a privilege.

When I see that iconic picture of three-year-old Syrian boy Aylan Kurdi drowned and washed up on a beach in Turkey as his family tried to reach Greece to escape the conflict, I find it impossible that anyone could actually refuse these people help. Just imagine! There are a host of others just like this family seeking asylum and we can give it! We have a chance to raise them up, to provide them a place to live, to shelter them from the storm. What an honor! What a privilege! What a chance to be a beacon of light on a day of dark skies!

I'm an American middle class white male. My life hasn't been trouble free, but I know that I've won the lottery of circumstances. Through none of my own doing, I sit atop the social ladder. It is my responsibility to offer a helping hand in every way I can to those on the lower rungs. It is my joy to be able to do it.

It's what I do every day at school. When I trudge to my car in the evening dark, I'm exhausted to the marrow of my bones. But I wouldn't have it any other way.

It's not uncommon for a student or two to see me on the way to my car, shout out my name with glee and give me an impromptu hug. At the end of the day, I know I've made a difference. I love being a teacher.

So if we're considering letting in more refugees, don't worry about me. Send them all my way. I'll take all you've got. That's what public schools do.

THE KILLER IN MY CLASSROOM

Some nights sleep just won't come.

I toss and turn, crumpling the blankets until I have to get up and read or pour myself a glass of water.

Sitting up in the pre-morning gloom, that's when they come back to me.

A parade of faces. No names. Words are all lost in the haze of time.

But the faces remain.

Kids I've taught and wondered about.

What ever happened to Jason? Did Rayvin ever get into dance school? I wonder if the army took Tyler ...

But there's one face that always comes last.

A strong straight lip. Soft nose. Brooding eyes.

Terrance ... Terrell ... TYRELL.

Yes. That's his name.

One of my first students. One of my biggest failures.

And I don't have to wonder what happened to him. I know with a dread of certainty.

He never got to play professional basketball like he wanted. He never even made it out of high school.

No, not dead – though I do have I gaggle of ghosts on my class rosters.

He's a murderer. Life in prison.

I was his 8th grade language arts teacher. It was my first year teaching in the district.

I had a reputation for being able to relate with hard-to-reach kids so they put me in the alternative education classroom.

I had a bunch of students from grades 6-8 who simply couldn't make it in the regular school setting.

These were kids with undiagnosed learning disabilities, appalling home environments, and/or chips on their shoulders that could cut iron.

But I loved it.

I taught the Read 180 curriculum – a plan designed for students just like mine. We had three stations – silent reading, computer remediation, and small group instruction.

The class was divided into three groups – students rotated through each group. Though I somehow monitored the whole thing, I spent most of my time meeting with kids in small group instruction.

I had an aide who helped the whole thing run smoothly, too. Lots of planning time, support and resources.

Every day was exhausting. I could barely stay awake on the

ride home. But it was worth it, because I felt like I was making a difference.

And there was Tyrell.

Few days went by without at least one of the children having to be disciplined. Sometimes it was just a simple redirection or even standing in close proximity to kids who seemed set to explode. Other times it was a brief one-on-one counseling session to find out why someone was misbehaving. And sometimes it was so bad kids had to be sent to the office. Once we even had a child escorted out of the building in handcuffs because he brought a weapon to class.

If you'd told me one of those children would end up killing someone, I wouldn't have blinked. If you told me it would be Tyrell, I wouldn't have believed you.

He was a gentle giant.

Almost always calm and in control. He was well above the others academically. When one of the others lost his cool, Tyrell would help talk him down.

I wondered why he was there. Turns out he was involved in a bloody fight on the way home from school the year before.

But that rarely made its way into the classroom. It was like he was already doing time – serving out his sentence with these misfits until he could be placed back with the rest of the student population.

I remember when Carlos got caught with the knife. Tyrell's back had stiffened but he hadn't moved.

The knife had fallen from Carlos' pocket across the table and slid to the floor.

Tyrell watched it slide across his desk but said nothing.

"Is that a knife, Carlos?" I asked.

"No!" he said picking it up and putting it back in his pocket.

"Why do you have a knife, Carlos?" I asked.

He shrugged and refused to say anything.

Then Tyrell spoke up.

"It's for the walk home, Mr. Singer."

"What?" I asked.

"He needs it," Tyrell said.

And the look in both of their eyes said it was true.

But what could I do? If he used that knife, I'd be liable.

I had to report it, and I did.

Would I still do that? Was it a mistake?

I don't know.

But I went to the administration and told them the truth – that I BELIEVED the knife was for self-defense. That something had to be done to protect these kids on the walk home.

Nothing changed. Our district saves a ton of money by forgoing buses. Richer kids get a ride to school. Poorer kids walk.

And Carlos got charged.

Tyrell never said anything about it. But I wondered what we'd find if we searched **HIM**.

We have metal detectors, but they are far from 100%.

I remember one day Tyrell stayed after class to talk to me. Talk quickly turned from grades and assignments to what he wanted to do with his life.

Tyrell loved B-ball. Often wore a Kobe jersey to school. And always the cleanest, brightest Jordans on his feet.

He was going to play ball, he said. No doubt about it.

I tried to convince him to have a backup plan, but he just shook his head.

"What kind of options you think there is out there for a guy like me, Mr. Singer?"

I'll never forget it. Me trying to convince him he could do anything he wanted, and he just smiling.

"Guy like me only do one of two things," he said, "He plays some ball or he runs out on the streets."

I asked him to explain, and he told me about his brothers – how they sold drugs, bought fancy cars, took care of the family.

I kept insisting there was another way – a better way. And finally he agreed but said that his way was easier, safer, more of a sure thing.

"Why should I work my ass off on all this?" he said pointing to his books, "I can make a stack on the street."

Was there anything I could have said to change his mind?

I don't know. But I tried.

And that was it, really. I never had another chance. They moved him back to regular ed. a few weeks later.

He finished the year with a different teacher in a different part of the building.

I saw him occasionally, and he'd dap me up, but that was about it.

The next year there was an opening for me in regular ed., too.

Eighth grade with the academic track population.

I had to really think about it. My colleagues thought I was crazy not jumping on it at the first opportunity.

But it was no easy decision.

What finally pushed me over the edge was the rumor that alternative ed. was being downsized.

They would no longer pay for the Read 180 curriculum. No more aides. No more resources and extra planning time.

So I put in for the move and have been there ever since.

Of course, with a much reduced alternative ed. most of the students I would have taught had moved up with me to the regular ed. classroom. Now they're just bunched in with the regular student population.

But I don't regret it. I love these kids. I love being there for them.

And Tyrell? About a year later, I read about him in the newspaper.

Police think it was a drug related hit. Tyrell was in the backseat. He put his gun to the driver's head and pulled the trigger.

Bam.

No more future for either of them.

Except on restless nights when Tyrell's face keeps coming back to me.

Is there something I could have done? Do the words exist for me to have convinced him to change his path? Would he have listened if I hadn't reported Carlos?

And most importantly – why am I the only one who seems to care?

PART II

SCHOOL CHOICE

TOP 10 REASONS SCHOOL CHOICE IS NO CHOICE

On the surface of it, school choice sounds like a great idea.

Parents will get to shop for schools and pick the one that best suits their children.

Oh! Look, Honey! This one has an exceptional music program! That one excels in math and science! The drama program at this one is first in the state!

But that's not at all what school choice actually is.

In reality, it's just a scam to make private schools cheaper for rich people, further erode the public school system, and allow for-profit corporations to gobble up education dollars meant to help children succeed.

Here's why:

1) Voucher programs almost never provide students with full tuition.

Voucher programs are all the rage, especially among conservatives. Legislation has been proposed throughout the country taking a portion of the tax dollars that would normally go to a public school and allowing parents to put it toward tuition at a private or parochial school. However, the cost of going to these schools is much higher than going to public schools. So even with your voucher tax dollars in hand, you don't have the money to go to these schools.[19]

For the majority of impoverished students attending public schools, vouchers don't help. Parents still have to find more money somewhere to make this happen. Poor folks just can't afford it. But rich folks can so let's reduce their bill!? They thank you for letting them buy another Ferrari with money that should have gone to help poor and middle class kids get an education.

2) Charter and voucher schools don't have to accept everyone

When you choose to go to one of these schools, they don't have to choose to accept you. In fact, the choice is really all up to them. Does your child make good grades? Is he or she well-behaved, in the special education program, learning disabled, etc.? If they don't like your answers, they won't accept you. They have all the power. It has nothing to do with providing a good education for your child.[20] It's all about whether your child will make them look good. By contrast, public schools take everyone and often achieve amazing results with the resources they have.

3) Charter Schools are notorious for kicking out hard to teach students

Charter schools like to tout how well they help kids learn. But they also like to brag that they accept diverse students. So they end up accepting lots of children with special needs at the beginning of the year and then giving them the boot before standardized test season.[21] That way, these students' low scores won't count against the charter school's record. They can keep bragging about their high test scores without actually having to expend all the time and energy of actually teaching[22] difficult students. Only public schools take everyone and give everyone their all.

4) Voucher and charter schools actually give parents less choice than traditional public schools

Public schools are governed by different rules than charter and voucher schools. Most public schools are run by a school board made up of duly-elected members from the community. The school board is accountable to that community. Residents have the right to be present at votes and debates, have a right to access public documents about how their local property tax money is being spent, etc. None of this is true at most charter or voucher schools.[23] They are run by executive boards or committees that are not accountable to parents. If you don't like what your public school is doing, you can organize, vote for new leadership or even take a leadership role yourself. If you don't like what your charter or voucher school is doing, your only choice is to withdraw your child. See ya!

5) Charter Schools do no better and often much worse than traditional public schools

Pundits and profiteers love to spout euphoric about how well charter schools teach kids. But there is zero evidence behind it.[24] That is nothing but a marketing ploy. It's like when you're in a bad neighborhood and walk past a dive that claims to have the best cup of coffee in the city. Yuck. Surely, some charter schools do exceptionally well. However, most charters and almost all cyber charters[25] do worse than their public school counterparts. Fact.

6) Charters and voucher schools increase segregation

Since the 1950s and '60s, we used to understand there was no such thing as separate but equal education. Before then we had Cadillac schools for white kids and broken down schools for black kids. The Supreme Court ruled that unconstitutional. But today we have Cadillac schools for rich and middle class kids – most of whom are white – and broken down schools for the poor – most of whom are black or brown. After making tremendous strides to integrate schools and provide an excellent education for everyone, our public schools have become increasingly resegregated. Charter and voucher schools only make this problem worse.[26] Depending on the district, they either help the white students escape, leaving students of color behind, or they leach away minority students leaving the white kids in the traditional district. Either way, they keep the races separate.[27] This just makes it easier to give some kids a leg up while keeping others down.

7) Charter and voucher schools take away funding at traditional public schools

It costs almost the same amount of money to run a school building of a given size regardless of the number of kids in it. When students leave the public schools for charter or voucher schools, the public school loses valuable resources. It now has less revenue but the same overhead.[28] So even if you found an excellent charter or voucher school to send your child to, you would be hurting the chances of every other student in the public school of having their own excellent education. This is what happens when you make schools compete for resources. Someone ends up losing out on an education, and that someone is invariably a minority, impoverished, or otherwise disadvantaged student.

8) Properly funding parallel school systems would be incredibly wasteful and expensive

We could fix this problem by providing adequate funding for all levels of the school system – traditional public schools, charter schools, voucher schools, etc. However, this would be exorbitantly expensive. We don't adequately fund our schools now. Adding extra layers like this would mean increasing national spending exponentially – maybe by three or four times the current level. And much of that money would go to waste. Why have three fully stocked school buildings in one community when one fully stocked building would do the job? I don't imagine residents would relish the tax hike this would require.

9) School choice takes away attention from the real problems in our public schools – poverty and funding equity

We have real problems. More than half of public school students live below the poverty line.[29] They are already several grade levels behind their non-impoverished peers before they even enter kindergarten. They need help – tutoring, counseling, wraparound services, nutrition, etc.[30] The predicament is even more complicated by the way we fund our schools. Throughout the country, poor districts get less money than wealthy or middle class ones. The students who go to these schools in poor school districts are systematically being cheated out of resources and opportunities. And instead of helping them, we're playing a shell game with charter and voucher schools. The problem isn't that parents don't have several excellent choices. If they're poor, they often don't have one.

10) School choice is not supported by a grass roots movement. It is supported by billionaires.

The proponents of school choice will tell you that they are only doing the will of the people. This is what parents want, they say. Baloney. While there are individuals who support school choice, the overwhelming majority of money behind this movement comes from conservative billionaires actively trying to dismantle the public education system. They want to steal the public system and replace it with a private one. They don't care about your child. They just want to steal the hundreds of billions of tax dollars we pay to educate our children. This is not philanthropy. It is a business transaction meant to screw you and your child out of your rights.

If we really want to ensure every child in this country gets an excellent education, the answer isn't school choice. Instead, we need to commit to supporting our public school systems. We all need to be in this together. Yes, our schools should look at the needs of each child and tailor education to fit appropriately. But that shouldn't be done in parallel school systems. It should be done under the same umbrella. That way, you can't defund and defraud one without hurting all. It can't just be about your child. It has to be about *all* children.

That's the only choice worth making.

WHY SCHOOLS SHOULD NOT BE RUN LIKE BUSINESSES

America loves business.

We worship the free market. Nothing is more infallible – not reason, not morals, not even God.

Money is the true measure of success – the more you have, the better a person you are.

This perverted ideology has taken over much of American life. Where we once cared about our country, justice and fair play, today it has all been reduced to dollars and cents.

Every problem can be answered by business. Every endeavor should be made more business-like. Every interaction should be modeled on the corporate contract, and every individual should try to maximize the outcome in his or her favor. Doing so is not just good for you personally, but it's what's best for everyone involved. And this dogma is preached by the high priests of the market, who claim that as they themselves get wealthier, one day we too will reap the same rewards. But that day never seems to come.

These principles are articles of faith so deeply ingrained that some folks can't see past them. They have become the driving force behind our country and much of the world. Meanwhile, as the privileged and advantaged few get ever wealthier, the majority of people get ever poorer. Our environment gets increasingly polluted, and everything is up for sale.

One of the last holdouts against this market-driven nightmare is the public school system.

We still have widespread educational institutions run democratically at public expense, dedicated to providing every child with the tools and opportunities to learn.

They're not perfect. Far from it. But they enshrine one of the last vestiges of the America of our grandparents. Democracy and justice are the system's core values – not profit, expansion and market share.

However, our schools suffer from disinvestment. Since we've segregated the rich in their private enclaves from the poor in impoverished neighborhoods, it's easy to provide more funding and resources to wealthy children and less to poor ones. That's the main reason why some schools struggle – they haven't the resources of the Cadillac institutions. Whenever we look at school spending, we look at an average allotment never bothering to consider that most of that money goes to the children of the wealthy, and much less goes to poor kids. Nor do we consider that more than half of our public school students live below the poverty line. Public schools strive to overcome the barriers of poverty, but the way we fund them ensures many of them are burdened by these same factors.

To make matters worse, our federal and state governments have allowed huge corporations to profit off our schools through an industry based on constant standardized testing which then sells schools the remediation materials to help students pass those same tests. That's all Common Core is, a more efficient way to market text books and test preparation materials regardless of their inherent value – or lack thereof – to students. The same people criticizing public schools for being untouched by a business ethic often ignore how much those schools have already been brutalized by free market capitalism and the profit motive.

In any case, despite all these encumbrances, these problems are all surmountable. Doing so only requires us to go in the opposite direction away from the boardroom and the Wall Street subprime bubble. We need to work intrinsically for the good of each student. We need to see well educated students as ends in themselves, and not just for how much profit they can be used to generate – not only while they are students, but also after they have been "educated" to fulfil the needs of the business world.

Unfortunately, such a solution is inconceivable to those in power. It goes against everything in which they believe. Too many Americans have been converted to the cult of the market so that the only solution they can support is to double down on what's not working – to turn public schools even further into a business.

It's absurd. Not everything benefits from being sold for a profit. Imagine if your spouse suggested running your marriage that way. It would turn you both into prostitutes selling yourselves at ever cheaper rates while any self-respect, dignity and love disappeared.

Some things just are not for sale. Would you give up your deepest held convictions because doing so might help you turn a profit? Today I'm not a Christian, I believe in Baal because he's got a bigger market share. Today I'm skeptical about gravity because the Acme Parachute Company is offering a bonus to jump out of the tenth floor naked.

Only fools let themselves be manipulated in this way. And that's exactly what corporations and big business are trying to do with our public schools. Make no mistake. These are *our* institutions – they belong to us – yet privateers see a way to gobble up tax dollars while downgrading the services provided. They want to play us all for suckers even if it means leaving the next generation of poor and middle class children in the lurch. The only thing that matters to them is making profits.

They say we should run schools like a business? What kind of business exactly?

There are many different kinds of free enterprise. A coal company runs much differently from a restaurant, for example.

Public schools are nothing like any for-profit business. Sure, historically we've had a small percentage of private schools, but our country has never survived on an education system that is wholly private. By definition, the model does not work for everyone. That's what the term "private" means – belonging to one person or group and not another. Our schools traditionally serve everyone. No single business in the country does that day-in-day-out. Perhaps we could find some new paradigm that would fit public schools, but let's not pretend we can take some business model that already exists and apply it willy-nilly. At the start, this mindset is naive at best.

Second, most businesses fail.

Most public schools succeed.[31] They have a proven track record. Why are we going to jump to a model that builds its success on the failure of competitors?

Competition means there will be winners and losers. That's fine in sports. It's even fine in most goods and services. There's not so much at stake. If I go to a bad restaurant, I have a bad meal. No big deal. I just go somewhere else tomorrow. If I get a bad education, there is no do over. I'm screwed.

That's just not acceptable. Would you bet your life on opening a new restaurant? Would you bet your child's education? Schools might not live up to your expectations, but at least the system isn't set up from the outset so that some of them will eventually crash and burn.

Third, businesses get to choose their raw materials.[32] If you're making pizzas, you buy the best grains, cheese, tomatoes, etc. But public schools don't get to choose their students. They have to teach even those who are more difficult to instruct. They accept kids with special needs, kids who've been abused, who live in poverty, who are undernourished, etc. And that's how it needs to be.

If we were to follow the typical business model where the goal is merely profit, we would try to find ways to weed out these difficult students and make them someone else's problem. In fact, that's exactly what many privately-run charter schools and vouchers schools do. If they want our tax dollars, they shouldn't be allowed to discriminate against our children. We should be seeking to stop such nefarious practices, not encourage them.

Finally, businesses are not essentially democratic. Corporations are beholden to their shareholders and businesses are beholden to their founders. Who, exactly, fits that role if we model our school after a business?

Public schools are run by democratically elected school boards. Privately run charter and voucher schools often are run by appointees. They aren't beholden to the public who provide the tax dollars they need to operate. They are beholden to the limited group of people who will profit from them economically.

This is a terrible model for public schools. It gives very little back to the taxpayer. It gives less value to the student.

Should we run our schools like businesses? Not if we value students and taxpayers more than the handful of investors looking to profit off our dime.

THE RACISTS ROOTS AND RACIST INDOCTRINATION OF SCHOOL CHOICE

"Simple justice requires that public funds, to which all taxpayers of all races contribute, not be spent in any fashion which encourages, subsidizes, or results in racial discrimination."

President John F. Kennedy

"Injustice anywhere is a threat to justice everywhere."

Dr. Martin Luther King, Jr.

Billionaires and far right policymakers are pushing for school choice.

I say they're pushing for it because voters always turn it down.[33]

Every single referendum held on school choice in the

United States has been defeated despite billions of dollars in corporate-backed spending to convince people[34] to vote for it.

But advocates aren't discouraged that the public isn't on their side. They have money, and in America that translates to speech.

The Trump administration is dedicated to making our public schools accept this policy whether people want it or not.

But don't think that's some huge change in policy. The previous administration championed a lighter version of these market-driven plans.[35] The main difference goes like this. Democrats are for charter schools and tax credits for private and parochial schools. Republicans are for anything that calls itself a school that is getting its hands on your tax dollars – charter schools, private schools, religious schools – if some charlatan opens a stand on the side of the road with the word "school" in the title, they get tax dollars.

In all this rush to give away federal and state money, no political party really champions traditional public schools, yet ninety percent of children attend them. In opinion polls, a majority of Americans like their local community schools. But like most things Americans want, politics goes the other way. Universal healthcare? Have Romney Care. Universal background checks on all gun sales? Nah. That sort of thing.

However, what often gets lost in the rush of politicians cashing in on this policy is its racist roots.

You read that right. School choice was invented as a mechanism of white flight[36] Before the federal government forced schools to desegregate, no one was all that interested in having an alternative to traditional public schools. But once whites got wind that the Supreme Court might make their kids go to school with black kids, lots of white parents started clamoring for "choice."

It was intended as a way to get around Brown vs. Board of Education. In 1953, a year before that landmark decision, many white southerners felt it was vitally important to continue a segregated education. They deeply desired to continue having "separate but equal" schools for the races, yet the U.S. Supreme Court seemed ready to strike that down.

Enter Georgia's Gov. Herman Talmadge who created what became known as the "private-school plan." [37] Talmadge proposed an amendment to the Georgia Constitution to empower the general assembly to privatize the state's public education system. "We can maintain separate schools regardless of the U.S. Supreme Court by reverting to a private system, subsidizing the child rather than the political subdivision," Talmadge said.

The plan goes like this. If the Supreme Court mandates desegregation – as it did – the state would close the public schools and issue vouchers allowing students to enroll in segregated private schools.

Fortunately, Talmadge's plan was never implemented in Georgia. But it became the model for segregationists everywhere.

In Prince Edward County, Virginia, the plan actually came to fruition – sort of.

Two years before the 1959 federal desegregation deadline, local newspaper publisher J.Barrye Wall explained what county leaders were planning[38]:

We are working [on] a scheme in which we will abandon public schools, sell the buildings to our corporation, reopen as privately operated schools with tuition grants from [Virginia] and P.E. county as the basic financial program ... Those wishing to go to integrated schools can take their tuition grants and operate their own schools. To hell with 'em.

Ultimately the county refused to sell the public school buildings. However, public education in Prince Edward County was nevertheless abandoned for five years, from 1959 to 1964. During that time, taxpayer dollars were funneled to the segregated white academies, which were housed in privately owned facilities such as churches and the local Moose Lodge.

The federal government struck down the program as a misuse of taxpayer funds after only a year, but even so whites benefited and blacks lost. Since there were no local taxes collected to operate public schools during those years, whites could invest in private schools for their children, while blacks in the county were left to fend for themselves. Since they were unable and unwilling to finance their own private, segregated schools, many black children were simply shut out of school for multiple years.

In other states, segregationists enacted "freedom of choice" plans that allowed parents of white students to transfer them out of desegregated schools. Any parents of black students that tried to do the same had to clear numerous administrative hurdles. Moreover, entering formerly all-white schools would subject them to harassment from teachers and students. Anything to keep the races apart in the classroom – and usually the entire building.

Eventually, segregationists began to realize that separate black and white schools would no longer be tolerated by the courts, so they had to devise other means to eliminate these "undesirables."

Attorney David Mays, who advised high-ranking Virginia politicians on school strategy, reasoned: [38]

Negroes could be let in [to white schools] and then chased out by setting high academic standards they could not maintain, by hazing if necessary, by economic pressures in some cases, etc. This should leave few Negroes in the white schools. The federal courts can easily force Negroes into our white schools, but they can't possibly administer them and listen to the merits of thousands of bellyaches.

Mays turned out to be somewhat prescient. Though desegregation efforts largely succeeded at first, in the last 20-30 years whites accomplished through housing and neighborhood segregation what they couldn't legally enforce through outright school segregation.[39] District lines were drawn to minimize the number of blacks at predominantly white schools and vice versa. Moreover, since funding was often tied to local property taxes, whites could legally ensure black schools got fewer resources than white schools. And with standardized tests constantly showing students at these schools as failing, policymakers could just blame the schools and the teachers instead of what they'd done to set the school up for failure.

Today racist policies undermine much of the structure of our public schools. We should acknowledge this and work to peel it back. We need to ensure all schools are equitably funded, that class sizes are under control, that all students get both a broad curriculum and the services they need. But in the absence of a new, robust desegregation policy, our schools will always be in danger of racist programs that can easily select which students to benefit and which to ignore.

Instead of doing this hard work, we're engaged in resurrecting the school choice policies of the deep South and universalizing them across the country. School vouchers are extremely similar to Talmadge's private school plan. The main difference is that vouchers don't close public schools outright, they simply allow them to be defunded and ignored. With universal school vouchers, public schools often become the *de facto* holding area for whichever group of children the private schools refuse to accept or who can't afford private school tuition even with the vouchers.

Charter schools are built on the Prince Edward County model of the early 1960s. They're administered as private institutions yet claim to be somehow public. As a result, they're allowed to bypass many of the rules that protect students at public schools from discrimination and fraud. In effect, they're largely unregulated. In the modern age, that means they can be incredibly substandard for long periods of time and no one knows or intervenes. The kinds of scandals perpetrated at some charter schools are simply not possible at traditional public schools. Some charters close without notice, have facilities used as nightclubs, involve taxpayer funds used for non-school purposes such as apartments for mistresses, the purchase of yachts, etc.

In both cases, charters and voucher schools often cater to mostly one race rather than another. That increases segregation at both these facilities and the traditional public schools. But voucher schools can go a step further. They can even put racism on the curriculum.

Supporting the racial order is often what's actually being taught at private and religious schools. They are infamous for revisionist history and denying climate science. What's less well-known is how they often try to normalize racist attitudes.

The American Christian Education (ACE) group provides fundamentalist school curriculum to thousands of religious schools throughout the country. Included in this curriculum is the A Beka Book and Bob Jones University Press textbooks.

A Beka publishers, in particular, reported that about 9,000 schools nationwide purchase their textbooks.[40]

These books include the following gobsmackers:

1. "[The Ku Klux] Klan in some areas of the country tried to be a means of reform, fighting the decline in morality and using the symbol of the cross. Klan targets were bootleggers, wife-beaters, and immoral movies. In some communities it achieved a certain respectability as it worked with politicians."[41]

   United States History for Christian Schools, 3rd ed., Bob Jones University Press, 2001

2. "God used the Trail of Tears to bring many Indians to Christ."[41]

   America: Land That I Love, Teacher ed., A Beka Book, 1994

3. "A few slave holders were undeniably cruel. Examples of slaves beaten to death were not common, neither were they unknown. The majority of slave holders treated their slaves well."[41]

   United States History for Christian Schools, 2nd ed., Bob Jones University Press, 1991

4. "To help them endure the difficulties of slavery, God gave Christian slaves the ability to combine the African heritage of song with the dignity of Christian praise. Through the Negro spiritual, the slaves developed the patience to wait on the Lord and discovered that the truest freedom is from the bondage of sin. By first giving them their spiritual freedom, God prepared the slaves for their coming physical freedom."[40]

Michael R. Lowman, George Thompson, and Kurt Grussendorf, United States History: Heritage of Freedom, 2nd ed. (Pensacola, FL: A Beka Book, 1996), p. 219.

5. "Africa is a continent with many needs. It is still in need of the gospel ... Only about ten percent of Africans can read and write. In some areas the mission schools have been shut down by Communists who have taken over the government."[41]

Old World History and Geography in Christian Perspective, 3rd ed., A Beka Book, 2004

6. Gay people "have no more claims to special rights than child molesters or rapists."[41]

Teacher's Resource Guide to Current Events for Christian Schools, 1998-1999, Bob Jones University Press, 1998

7. Brown v. Board of Education is described as social activism by the Supreme Court: "While the end was a noble one – ending discrimination in schools – the means were troublesome ... liberals were not willing to wait for a political solution."[40]

Teacher's Resource Guide to Current Events for Christian Schools, 1998 – 1999 (Greenville, SC: Bob Jones University Press, 1998), p. 34

These are claims that are uncritically being taught to children at many voucher schools. If this were happening only at private schools, it would be troubling that racists were indoctrinating their children in the same hatred and bigotry of their parents. However, that we're actually using public money – and planning to expand the amount of public money – to increase the racism and prejudice of the next generation is beyond troubling! It's infuriating!

School choice does not enhance civil rights. It is inimical to them. It is part of a blatant policy to make America racist again. We cannot allow the Trump administration and any neoliberal Democrats who quietly support his ends to undo all the progress we've made in the last 60 years.

The bottom line is this – voters don't want school choice. It does nothing to better children's educations. It is a product of segregation and racism, and even in its modern guise it continues to foster segregation and racism.

If we care about civil rights, social equality and democratic rule, school choice is something that should be relegated to the dust heap of history. It's time to move forward, not look back fondly on the Confederacy, Jim Crow and segregationism.

SCHOOL VOUCHERS - TRANSUBSTANTIATE YOUR CASH FOR FUN AND PROFIT

When is a tax dollar not a tax dollar?

When it's used to pay for a school voucher.

That's the sleight of hand behind much of our education policy today.

Lawmakers want to give away a huge bundle of your cash to religious schools, but they can't because of that pesky old First Amendment.

The establishment clause sets up a distinct separation between church and state. It explicitly forbids public money being spent on any specific religion.

So these lawmakers do a bit of magic. They take that money, wave their hands over it, mumble a few secret words and *Voilà*! It's no longer public, it's private. And private money can be spent any way you want – even on religion.

Here's how they do it.

You simply take public tax dollars and turn them into credits that can be used to pay for alternatives to public schools. Call it a "school voucher."

But wait a minute. Isn't that like a check? If Peter writes Paul a check, that money is no longer Peter's. Now it's Paul's. Right?

Yes. But that's not what's happening here.

A school voucher isn't a check. A check is an order to your bank to transfer funds to another account or to be exchanged for cash, goods or services. School vouchers do not come from your account. And they cannot be transferred into just any account or spent in any way.

They're more like food stamps. It's not money that can be used in any way you see fit. It's money that can only be used to pay for a child's education. And you can only use it at a private or parochial school.

You can't go into a fancy restaurant and buy a filet mignon dinner with food stamps. Likewise, you can't go to a real estate developer and buy a house using your school vouchers.

This money does not therefore change from public to private. Yes, individuals get a limited choice of how this money will be spent, but that's true of all public money. Go to a local council meeting, a school board meeting, write your Congressperson, petition your state Senator – in all of these cases, you are exercising choice on how public tax dollars are being spent. *Don't spend tax dollars on that bridge. Don't spend public money on that program.*

Even in the case of food stamps, individuals decide how public dollars are spent for your private use – within specified limits.

If that was really private money, there would be no restrictions on how it could be spent – or certainly no more restrictions than on any other private money.

But lawmakers are pretending like this isn't true. They're pretending that simply changing the name of the money changes its substance. It's a lie. It's sleight of hand. They're trying to trick you into assuming a transformation has taken place that has not.

BAD DEAL

Moreover, it's a metamorphosis we shouldn't want in the first place.

We want our public money spent in an accountable fashion. We want there to be a record of how it was spent and what it was spent on. We want that information to be readily available, and if that money was misappropriated, we want to be able to act on that.

School vouchers remove much of that accountability. Private and parochial schools simply don't provide the same transparency as traditional public schools. Often there is no elected school board, no public meetings, no open documents. Nada.

But if the parents who used the school voucher don't like how the money is being spent, they can dis-enroll their child, right? So if they're comfortable without this transparency, that's all that matters, right?

Wrong. School vouchers are not paid for 100% by the parent. They are paid for with an aggregation of local tax dollars above and beyond what individual parents pay in school taxes.

In short, this is not just your money even if it's spent on

your kid. You shouldn't be the only one who gets a say in how this money is spent. The community provided this money. The community should decide how it's spent. At very least, the community should get a say.

If the community doesn't want children to be raised with a distinctly Biblical view of history and science, the community shouldn't have to contribute to that. If individual parents want to spend their own money on that, fine. That's their prerogative. But school vouchers are made up of public tax dollars, yet we're removing the majority of the public from having a voice in how that money is spent.

Moreover, traditional public schools are required not to discriminate against students. They can't select against students based on learning disabilities, ethnicity, skin color, gender, religion, sexual orientation, etc. And that's a really good thing. Everyone's money is used to pay for these schools. These schools should serve everyone.

But private and parochial schools – and charter schools, too, by the way – aren't held to this same standard. It's telling, for example, that U.S. Secretary of Education Betsy DeVos has refused to commit to holding private and parochial schools that accept school vouchers accountable if they discriminate against children. She seems to be implying that the U.S. government will stand aside and let public tax dollars be spent to support schools that discriminate. And the reason they think they can get away with this is the cynical monetary alchemy outlined above – *school vouchers are private money and can be spent any way parents want.*

It isn't, and they can't.

This is government sanctioned money laundering, pure and simple.

Lawmakers have been bought off with huge donations from the privatization industry to enact legislation friendly toward private and parochial schools.

NAME CHANGE

In some cases, they don't even use the name "school vouchers." They call it education tax credit scholarships, but it's effectively the same thing.

Instead of distributing the vouchers directly to parents, they allow businesses and individuals to make tax deductible donations to nonprofits set up explicitly to distribute vouchers for private and parochial schools.

The reason? People don't like school vouchers. But if you call it a "scholarship," it's more palatable. For instance, while school vouchers are mostly supported by Republicans, a substantial number of Democrats support education tax credit scholarships.

In 17 states you can get substantial tax credits for donating to one of these private and parochial school scholarships:[42]

Louisiana, Oklahoma, Pennsylvania, Rhode Island, and Virginia, for example, all provide tax credits worth between $65 and $95 on every $100 donated. Alabama, Arizona, Georgia, Montana, and South Carolina go even further by providing dollar-for-dollar tax credits. Donate $100, and receive $100 back in tax credits.

You read that right. Donate $100, get $100 back. Oh, but it gets much worse. Since these are considered donations, you can also claim them as charitable deductions and get an additional 35% off your taxes. So you donate $100 and get back $135! Yes! You actually make money off this deal!

In my home state of Pennsylvania, investors can even "triple dip" receiving a state tax credit, a reduction in their state taxable income, and a reduction in their federal taxable income. And, yes, that means they sometimes get back more in tax breaks than they provide in contributions.

Meanwhile all of these "savings" come from money stolen from local public schools. Businesses and individual investors are profiting off of the deteriorating conditions at public schools.

Ever wonder why class sizes are ballooning, teachers are being furloughed and electives are falling by the wayside? It's because people are making money off children's suffering.

In the Keystone state, we call this the Opportunity Scholarship Tax Credit (OSTC) and the Educational Improvement Tax Credit (EITC) programs.

The state Budget and Policy Center estimates[43] that about 76% of these "scholarships" go to religious schools. That was approximately $95 million dollars in 2014-15, the last year for which data was available.

Many of these educational institutions are explicitly fundamentalist. This includes the 155 schools in the Association of Christian Schools International (ASCI) where they boast of "the highest belief in biblical accuracy in scientific and historical matters." It also includes 35 schools in the Keystone Christian Education Association.

How many more parochial schools are using tax dollars to teach fundamentalist curriculum? Without an audit, we'll never know.

And that's a really significant issue.

These scholarships are supposed to be eligible only to low income students. Yet a significant number of them are being utilized at private schools with average tuitions of $32,000 – far more than the few thousand dollars provided by the scholarships. They are apparently being used by wealthy and middle class students who can already afford private schools but are using public tax dollars to reduce the cost.

A total of $11.2 million in EITC and OSTC tax credits in Pennsylvania went to just 23 of the most exclusive and expensive private schools in 2014-15, according to the state Budget and Policy Center. That's 9% of the total. Suburban Philadelphia's Haverford School, alone, received $2.2 million, buying down its $37,500 tuition.

How many parents misused these scholarships in this way? What is the racial and ethnic makeup of recipients? Again, without an audit, we don't know.

This is not how public money should be spent.

We need to put the brakes on these initiatives, not expand them into a federal incentive program as the Trump Administration proposes.

Whether you call them education tax credit scholarships or school vouchers, these programs do not transform public money into private.

They are a scam. They are theft. And their biggest victims are children.

SCHOOL VOUCHERS WILL INDOCTRINATE A GENERATION IN ALTERNATIVE TRUTHS

My middle school students are good at telling the difference between facts and opinions.

Facts, they'll tell you, are things that can be proven.

They don't even have to be true. They just have to be provable – one way or the other.

For instance – "I'm six feet tall." It's not true, but you could conceivably measure me and determine my height.

Opinions, on the other hand, are statements that have no way of being proven. They are value judgements. That is good. This is bad. Mr. Singer is short. Mr. Singer is tall.

It doesn't make them less important – in fact, their relative importance to facts is, itself, an opinion.

But today the very ability to prove facts has been called into question.

Our government has put forward statements that are demonstrably false. The Bowling Green Massacre. Undocumented immigrants commit massive amounts of crime. Donald Trump had the largest Electoral College victory of modern times.

All of these should objectively be viewed as facts. They're false, but they are provably false. Yet when we resort to the kinds of things that should count as proof, we refuse to agree, we come to a clash of epistemologies.

Today, your truth depends more on your political affiliation than your commitment to objective reality.

There was no Bowling Green Massacre. No one was killed in Bowling Green, Kentucky. Certainly there was no large scale mass death perpetrated by terrorists. There were two Iraqi nationals arrested who had been planning an attack outside of the U.S. They had been buying guns and materials here because they were easier to get.

However, many conservatives refuse to accept this. They believe there *was* a Bowling Green Massacre. And they believe that it justifies Trump's immigration ban.

The same goes for undocumented immigrants committing crime. They do **NOT** actually commit more crime than U.S. citizens.[44] In fact, they commit less. They don't want to attract unnecessary attention and risk deportation.

But once again many conservatives refuse to believe this. With no hard evidence, maybe some anecdotal evidence blown way out of proportion, they simply accept what they're told by their government and their chosen media.

And Trump's Electoral College victory? He won 306 of 538 electoral votes and lost the popular vote.[45] Forty-five Presidents won by a greater margin. And only two Presidents have had a lower popular vote tally.

These are just numbers. I don't know how they're controversial or how anyone can disagree, but many conservatives do.

Don't get me wrong. Liberals do it, too, though to a lesser degree. Ask most liberals about President Barack Obama's education policy[46] and you'll get a gooey story about support and progressivism. It isn't true.

One popular meme shows Obama lecturing a tiny Trump about how he should invest in education and respect parents and teachers. Yet Obama never really did those things, himself. He held federal education funding hostage unless districts increased standardized testing, Common Core and charter schools. **THAT'S** not what parents and teachers wanted! It's what huge corporations wanted so they could profit off our public schools!

But to many liberals Obama is some kind of saint, and any evidence to the contrary will be accepted only with great reluctance.

THIS is our modern world. A world of alternative facts and competing narratives. Part of it is due to the Internet and the way knowledge has been democratized. Part of it is due to the media conglomerates where almost all traditional news is disseminated by a handful of biased corporations that slant the story to maximize their profits.

People end up picking the sources of information they think are trustworthy and shutting themselves off to other viewpoints. There is no more news. There is conservative news and liberal news. And the one you consume determines what you'll accept as a fact.

As bad as that is, Trump's education policy is poised to make it much worse.

He wants to radically increase the amount of school vouchers given to students. These allow federal dollars to be used to send children to private and parochial schools. As if the fly-by-night charter schools weren't enough.

It's a scam. A get rich quick scheme for corporations at the expense of students. But perhaps the worst part is how it exacerbates our world of alternative facts.

Students at private and parochial schools don't learn the same things as public school students. At many religious schools they are indoctrinated in conservative market theory and a Biblical view of history and science.

You think we can't agree on the truth or falsity of facts now? Just wait! What counts as a source will be radically different for the first generation of kids sent to such disparate schools.

This isn't just about cashing in on education dollars today. It's about creating a generation of adults educated with school vouchers who accept far right ideas about the world as bedrock truths – *Climate change and evolution are hoaxes. Trickle-down economics works. Slavery benefited slave and master alike.*

These are the false truths the Trump administration hopes to seed into a larger portion of the next generation. And when you indoctrinate children so young, there is little hope they'll ever be able to see beyond what they've been taught.

Conservatives counter that liberals are doing the same thing today in our public schools. That's why they want to send their children to the private and parochial schools. They don't want their kids taught about modern science without reference to God. They don't want them to learn history that puts socialistic policies in a positive light. They don't want them to learn that white people were ever inhumane to people of color.

And how do you argue with them? How do you have a productive conversation when you can't agree on what proves a fact true or false?

This is the challenge of our generation.

I don't know how to solve it, but I know that school vouchers will make it exponentially worse.

PART III

TESTING

U.S. PUBLIC SCHOOLS ARE NOT FAILING - THEY'RE AMONG THE BEST IN THE WORLD

Everyone knows U.S. public schools are failing.

Just like everyone knows you should never wake sleepwalkers, bulls hate red and Napoleon was short.

Wrong on all counts.[47] Waking sleepwalkers will cause them no harm – in fact, they're more likely to harm themselves while sleepwalking. Bulls are colorblind – they're attracted to movement. And Napoleon was 5'7", which was above average height for Frenchman during his lifetime.

So why do we believe that American public schools are doing such a terrible job?

Because far right policymakers have convinced us all that it's true.

It's not.

Let me repeat that in no uncertain terms – America's

public schools are NOT failing. They are among the best in the world.[48] Really!

Here's why – the United States educates everyone. Most other countries do not.

Despite systemic underfunding of poor and minority students, vulture industries earning billions of dollars as parasites off our public schools, and everything else – we do something few other national systems of public education even attempt. We have made a commitment to every single child regardless of what their parents can afford to pay, regardless of their access to transportation, regardless of whether they can afford uniforms, lunch or even if they have a home. Heck! We even provide education to children who are here illegally.

That can't be said of many countries with which we're often compared – especially countries comparable to the U.S. in size or diversity.[49] So from the get-go, even after you consider all the disadvantages of the American system, we come out near the top because we have an advantage over most of the world.

We define education differently. Though our laws are woefully backward, in practice we look at it as a right, not a privilege. And for a full 13 years – counting kindergarten – it's a right for every child, not just some.

But that's not all! We also provide some of the highest quality education you can get in the world! We teach more, help more, achieve more and yet we are criticized more than any system in any country in the world.

TEST SCORES

Critics argue that our scores on international tests don't justify such a claim[50]. But they're wrong before you even look at the numbers. They're comparing apples to pears. You simply can't compare the United States to countries that leave hundreds of thousands of rural and poor children without any education whatsoever. The Bates Motel may have the softest pillows in town, but it's immediately disqualified because of the high chance of being murdered in the shower.

No school system of this size anywhere in the world exceeds the United States in providing free access to education *for everyone*. And that, alone, makes us one of the best.

It doesn't mean our system is problem free. There are plenty of ways we could improve. We're still incredibly segregated by race and class. Our funding formulas are often regressive and inadequate. Schools serving mostly poor students don't have nearly the resources of those serving rich students. But at least at the very outset what we're trying to do is better than what most of the world takes on. You can't achieve equity if it isn't even on the menu.

However, for some people, this will not be enough. They'll say that despite our high ideals, the quality of what we actually provide our students is low. After all, those international test scores are so low.

First point – it depends on the scores you're looking at. American elementary and middle school students have improved on the Trends in International Mathematics and Science Study[51] every four years since the tests began in 1995. They are above the international average in all categories and within a few percentage points of the global leaders – something rarely mentioned on the nightly news.

Even on the PISA test administered by the Organization for Economic Cooperation and Development to 15-year-olds in about 60 countries, U.S. children are far from the bottom of the scale. We're somewhere in the middle.[52] We've always been in the middle for all the decades since they've been making these comparisons. Our schools have not gotten worse. They have stayed more or less the same.[53]

IDEALS AND POVERTY

To some this just demonstrates that our schools have always been mediocre. But again they're overlooking the consequences of our ideals.

The broader the spectrum of children who take a test, the lower the average score will be. In other words, if only your top students take the test, your average score will be very high. If only your top and middle students take the test, your average score still will be quite high. But if **ALL** of your students take the test, your average score will be lower.

Now add in poverty. Living in poverty reduces your access to health care, books, early childhood education and many other factors that increase learning throughout your life.[54] Children from poor families are already more than a year behind those of rich parents on the first day of kindergarten.[55] If you only test the wealthiest students, the average test score will probably be quite high. The average score will drop dramatically if you test all of your students.

That's why many of these countries where the poorest children do not have access to education have higher test scores than the United States. You're not comparing equals.[56] The United States has the highest child poverty rate in the Western World. And we don't hide those children away. We include them on our tests. That has a major impact on our scores. But talking heads on TV almost always ignore it. They pretend it doesn't exist. It's the only way they can use these test scores to "prove" to a gullible audience that America's schools are failing.

But if you fairly compare education systems and factor in the equal access we provide for all children to an education, our system comes out way on top. We have one of the best systems in the world.

But wait! There's more!

SPECIAL EDUCATION

Not only does the United States serve all children regardless of academic achievement or poverty. We also serve far more students with disabilities.

Why are there so many special education children in the U.S.? Because we have a higher standard of living.

A standard pregnancy lasts about 280 days or 40 weeks. However, some mothers give birth to children after only 28 weeks. Two decades ago, these babies would not have survived. Today, they often do. Five years later these children will enter kindergarten and our school system will be responsible for teaching them to read, write and learn math. In other countries, premature babies have a much lower chance of survival. They don't survive to become the special education population. So things as diverse as the live-birth rate actually affect average test scores.

Another counterintuitive factor is the suicide rate. In many countries where pressure to perform at the highest levels on standardized tests is extreme, many children are actually driven to suicide. This is especially true in numerous Asian countries with a record of high scores on the international tests.[57] So a higher suicide rate actually increases test scores.

Would you say this makes other countries superior to the United States? Heck no! In fact, just the opposite. I certainly wouldn't wish more underperforming U.S. students were ending their lives so we could do better on international tests. Nor would I wish that more premature babies died to improve our international standing.

We have developed a special education system to help children at the edges that many other countries just can't touch. In some countries these students are simply excluded. In others they are institutionalized. In some countries it's up to parents to find ways to pay for special services. The United States is one of the only countries where these children are not only included and offered full and free access, but the schools go above and beyond to teach these children well beyond their 13th academic year. In every public school in the United States these students are included. In math, reading, science and social studies, they are there benefiting from instruction with the rest of the class. And this, in turn, benefits even our non-special education students who gain lessons in empathy and experience the full range of human abilities.

Of course, most of our special education students are also included in our test scores. Yes, other countries that ignore these children and exclude them from testing get higher scores. But so what? Do you mean to tell me this makes them better? No, it makes them worse.

In many ways, we are the gold standard, not them. They should be emulating us, not the other way around. They should be jealous of the way we prize each other's humanity. We shouldn't be salivating at test scores achieved through shunning certain students in favor of others.

CURRICULUM AND STRATIFICATION

But it's not just who we teach, it's also what we teach.

Compared to many other countries, U.S. school curriculum is often much wider and varied.[58] Countries that focus only on test preparation and test results often leave out sciences, arts, literature and humanities.

Unfortunately, the push from policymakers even in the U.S. has been to narrow curriculum to imitate some of the worst practices of our competitors.[59] But in many districts we still strive to create well-rounded graduates and not just good test-takers.

The bottom line is that the curriculum at most American schools is more inclusive than that found internationally. We even include societal issues like alcohol and drug abuse prevention, stress reduction and relaxation, and physical fitness programs.

In addition we don't stratify our children based on academic ability to nearly the same degree as many international schools. We don't weed out our worst students through middle and high school until only our most capable are left in 12th grade. Nor is college only open to our best and brightest. We make a much greater effort than many other countries to keep this option open to as many students as possible regardless of whether they can afford it or not. The number of Americans with at least some college education has soared over the past 70 years,[60] from 10 percent in 1940 to 56 percent today, even as the population has tripled and the nation has grown vastly more diverse. Meanwhile, graduation rates are at an all-time high of 83.2 percent[61], and for the first time minority students are catching up with their white counterparts.

It's not easy. But it's something we're committed to as a nation. And that's not true around the world.

SIZE MATTERS

Finally, there's the issue of size. The United States is a big country – the third most populous in the world. According to the U.S. Census Bureau, We have 324,450,000 people and growing. That's about 50 million students in public schools, according to the National Center for Education Statistics.

It's much easier to educate fewer children. Even excellent education systems would struggle with our sheer numbers. Small systems often outshine bigger ones. For instance, I might be able to make dinner for my immediate family, but I'd find it much more challenging to prepare a meal for a banquet hall of hundreds. Similarly, it remains to be seen whether smaller nations could handle educating a population as big and diverse as ours without collapsing.

By any fair measure, America's public education system is simply stunning. But the media perpetuates the myth that we're failing.

PUBLIC PERCEPTION AND THE MEDIA

After decades of hearing these falsehoods, the American public is strikingly divided. On a 2011 Gallup poll,[62] parents were asked their opinion of their local school and the public was asked its opinion of schools in general. The results were enlightening. Parents who gave their local school an A grade were at the highest percentage ever – 37% – whereas only 1% of respondents rated the nation's schools that way. Why the difference? Respondents said it was mostly because people knew about their local schools through direct experience. They only learned about the state of education nationally through the news media.

Why is education reporting so biased? Part of it is monetary. Huge corporations make hundreds of millions of dollars from the failing schools narrative.[63] They sell new standardized tests, new test preparation materials, new Common Core books, training programs for teachers, materials, etc.[64] If they can't demonstrate that our schools are failing, their market shrinks. And who do you think owns the shrinking media conglomerates? That's right, many of these same corporations.

But even when journalists want to be fair, it's difficult for them to get the inside story on how our public schools work. They are rarely permitted inside our schools to see the day-to-day classroom experience. Legal issues about which students may be photographed, filmed or interviewed, the difficulty of getting parental permissions, and the possibility of embarrassment to principals and administrators often keeps the doors closed. In many districts, teachers aren't even allowed to speak on the record to the media, or doing so can make them a political target. So reporters are often in the position of being unable to directly experience the very thing they're reporting on. In the words of Washington Post reporter Paul Farhi, "Imagine if sportswriters never got to see athletes play or political reporters never attended a campaign rally"[65]. Of course there would be a disconnect!

So we're left with a public education system that should be the envy of the world being portrayed as a loser.

THE BOTTOM LINE

As ever, far right politicians on both sides of the aisle, whether they be Democratic Neoliberals or Republican Tea Partiers, are using falsehoods about our public schools to sell an alternative. They say our public schools are beyond saving and that we need to privatize. They call it school choice but it's really just an attempt to destroy the system that has so much going for it.

We should strengthen public education not undermine it. We should roll up our sleeves and fix the real problems we have, not invent fake ones.

People act as if "alternative facts" were invented by the Trump administration. Our policymakers have been using them for decades in a libelous and dishonest campaign against our public schools.

They are some of the best in the world – if only people knew it.

STANDARDIZED TESTS HAVE ALWAYS BEEN ABOUT KEEPING PEOPLE IN THEIR PLACE

There are some things that can't be unseen.

America's history of standardized testing is one of them.

Today, critics from all sides of the political spectrum decry the overuse of high stakes tests, while paradoxically championing them for accountability purposes – especially for schools serving minority students.

Civil rights organizations that last year opposed testing have suddenly come to demand it – not because testing ensures racial equity but for fear of losing wealthy donors tied to the assessment industry. [66]

Yet one look at where these tests come from and how they have been used in the past shows their essentially classist and racist natures.

Make no mistake – standardized testing has been a tool of social control for the last century. And it remains one today.

Twisted statistics, made up math, nonexistent or biased

research – these are the "scientific" supports for standardized testing. It has never been demonstrated that these kinds of tests can accurately assess either intelligence or knowledge,[67] especially as that knowledge gets more complex. But there is an unspoken agreement in political circles to pretend that testing is rock solid and produces scores that can be relied on to make decisions that will have tremendous effects on the lives of students, teachers, parents and communities.

Our modern assessments are holdovers from the 1910s and 1920s, an age when psychologists thought they could isolate the racial markers for intelligence and then improve human beings through selective breeding like you might with dogs or cats.

I'm not kidding.

It was called eugenics.

Psychologists like Carl Brigham, Robert Yerkes, and Lewis Terman were trying to find a way to justify the social order. Why is it that certain people are at the top and others at the bottom? What is the best way to decide who belongs where?

To answer these questions they appealed to a radical misreading of Gregor Mendel and Charles Darwin.[68] They thought they had discovered something new about the human brain. Positive traits such as intelligence were widespread in Northwestern European races and almost nonexistent in others. Moreover, negative traits such as laziness and criminality were common in non-whites and almost absent in those same Northwestern Europeans.

It was really just the same kind of racial prejudices that have been prevalent throughout Europe for centuries, but now American pseudoscientists had found a justification for believing them. In fact, they argued that these deductions weren't prejudices at all.[69] They were facts based on evidence.

It was "science."

To make such conclusions they had to blind themselves to the effects of wealth and social class. The rich tend to be more well-behaved and educated than the poor. These psychologists took this to mean that the rich were somehow genetically superior. And since the rich were mostly of Northwestern European ancestry, they concluded their genes produced a racially superior type of human. They ignored the fact that a privileged upbringing bestows certain benefits, while an impoverished one inflicts life-altering wounds.[70] Ultimately, their "science" was simply a justification for their prejudices.

They came to many of these "discoveries" during the First World War. Yerkes developed the U.S. Army Alpha and Beta Intelligence tests that were given to almost all American soldiers. Ostensibly, the assessments were used to determine where soldiers were best suited – support services, the trenches, the officer core, etc.

The rationale was to ensure these assignments were being given more fairly and objectively. Before these tests, soldiers were assigned based on wealth and class. Now soldiers were assigned based on tests – that supported the exact same assignments based on wealth and class.

Until this point, IQ tests had to be given by one highly trained proctor to one person at a time. Yerkes' advancement was to put it all on paper so that multiple people could take the tests at the same time.

However, the tests were deeply flawed. Yerkes claimed they showed a person's natural intelligence. But the questions were clearly assessing knowledge of facts like a 1900s version of trivial pursuit.

For instance, here is Question 18 of the Alpha Test:[71]

"Velvet Joe appears in advertisements of … (tooth powder) (dry goods)(tobacco)(soap)."

The answer is tobacco. How you could know that without having seen period advertisements is beyond me. In any case, it gave good cover for positioning white, affluent men as officers, while mostly darker complexioned and working class soldiers populated the trenches.

After the armistice, Yerkes and Brigham used the wartime test results to continue sorting and ranking Americans. They claimed that their assessments had shown a terrible danger for the human race – nearly half of the white draft (47.3%) was feeble-mind. The cause? Not enough exposure to print advertising? No. They were interbreeding with members of inferior genetic strains.

"No citizen can afford to ignore the menace of race deterioration," wrote Yerkes in 1922 in the introduction to Brigham's "A Study of American Intelligence".[72] In that same book, one of Brigham's most seminal, the author was even more specific – "American education is declining and will proceed … with an accelerating rate as the racial mixture becomes more and more extensive."

Something had to be done. Pure whites needed to be segregated from mongrel races. But how to do it without being accused of prejudice or bias? How to make it seem like science? Once again, the answer was standardized testing.

Brigham created a civilian test of intelligence that could be used to sort and rank students just as the Army Alpha and Beta tests had been used to sort soldiers. He called it the Scholastic Aptitude Test or S.A.T.

Yes, **THAT** SAT.

Though the test has been revised multiple times since

Brigham created it, the purpose has remained the same – to distinguish the wheat from the chaff, to hold some students up as worthy of further educational investment and to keep others out. Moreover, the means by which the SAT makes this distinction was and remains culturally and economically biased. Researchers have been pointing out since Brigham's day that the test favors students from wealthy, white backgrounds over those from poor minority homes.[73] Yet today 2.1 million teenagers every year still must take the test to get into the college of their choice.

And so eugenics became education policy throughout the country from primary to post-secondary school.

Terman, who created the Stanford-Binet Intelligence Test to identify "slow" children for special education programs, went on to champion rigid academic tracking for all students in public schools based on standardized testing. The idea was to give the racially pure students extra resources and keep the mixed or lower races in classes more suited to their lower intellects and eventual menial stations in life.[74]

It is sad that many of these ideas persist in our present-day schools. Even today, economically disadvantaged and minority students still make up the majority of remedial and academic classes, while the children of the middle class and the wealthy – most of whom incidentally are white – disproportionately populate the honors classes. Today we write that off as merely accidental if we think about it at all. However, a peek at history shows quite clearly that it is exactly how the system has been designed to work.

From these beginnings eugenics became the dominant American policy of social organization. It was a required course of study for all education majors at colleges and universities. It was the justification for our isolationist foreign policy allowing thousands of immigrants to be turned away for fear of watering down the U.S. gene pool. Even inside our own borders, tens of thousands of Americans were subjected to mandatory sterilization to ensure degenerate genes were eradicated. In fact, it wasn't until the end of WWII and the Nuremberg Trials when the eugenicist star began to fade.

We come to a difficult and painful chapter in American history. The word "Nazi" has become an overenthusiastic and easy pejorative for anything that critics wish to vilify. Godwin's Law states that almost any argument on the Internet will eventually degrade to one side calling the other Adolph Hitler.

He has a point. We should be careful. Too often we wield the sledgehammer of Nazism to smash anything we don't like. But we can't let it silence the truth. Sometimes a policy really is Nazism. And if eugenics isn't, I don't know what is.

Here it is from Hitler's Mein Kampf:[75]

There is today one state in which at least weak beginnings toward a better conception [of immigration] are noticeable. Of course, it is not our model German Republic, but the United States.

Hitler proudly told his comrades[76] just how closely he followed the progress of the American eugenics movement. "I have studied with great interest," he told a fellow Nazi, "the laws of several American states concerning prevention of reproduction by people whose progeny would, in all probability, be of no value or be injurious to the racial stock."

Hitler even wrote a fan letter[77] to American eugenic leader Madison Grant, calling his race-based eugenics book *The Passing of the Great Race* his "Bible."

And lest we forget, the U.S. based Rockefeller Foundation[78] helped found the eugenics program in Germany, and even funded the section that Josef Mengele worked in before he went to Auschwitz. By 1926, Rockefeller had donated some $410,000 – almost $4 million in 21st-Century money – to hundreds of German researchers. Without American funds, these programs could not have gotten off the ground.

Nazis even looked to the U.S. Supreme Court for inspiration. In 1927, the court decided in Buck v. Bell that mandatory sterilization of feeble-minded individuals was, in fact, Constitutional. The ruling, which has never been explicitly overturned, resulted in the forced sterilization of between 60,000 and 70,000 Americans.

In the Supreme Court's opinion, Justice Oliver Wendell Holmes wrote:[79]

> It is better for all the world, if instead of waiting to execute degenerate offspring for crime, or to let them starve for their imbecility, society can prevent those who are manifestly unfit from continuing their kind.... Three generations of imbeciles are enough.

The Nazis at the Nuremberg Trials repeatedly quoted Holmes's words in their own defense.

This is what finally tainted the eugenics brand beyond repair. Psychologists and policymakers didn't want to be associated with the horrors of the war. They didn't want any of the blame though they clearly deserved a portion of it. They inspired it.

It took almost two additional decades for these ideas to largely dissipate.[80] It wasn't until the 1960s and the Civil Rights movement when Americans began to question the social order and the educational system that helped preserve it.

Schools changed. Students were increasingly desegregated both racially and academically. Less emphasis was put on testing and sorting and more on experimentation and self-discovery. Creativity and original thinking were prized above all else. Things weren't perfect, but we had entered a new era that refused to put children into rigid boxes. They were all unique and valuable and should be treated as such. But it couldn't last.

Flash forward to 1983. President Ronald Reagan's National Commission on Excellence in Education put out a report called "A Nation at Risk." Like the eugenicist work of the 1910s and 1920s, it purported to "prove" that our public schools were failing. Something had to be done.

The answer was the same as that of the eugenicists. We needed more standardized tests. We needed to return to the practices of sorting and ranking students followed by rigid tracking.

It didn't matter that "A Nation at Risk" was just as flawed and biased[81] as Brigham's WWI data. It didn't matter that this same policy hadn't yielded superior academic results in the 1920s, 1930s and 1940s. It didn't matter that since we'd put an emphasis on desegregation and creativity, American education was producing unprecedented racial and economic equity. Politically, the only thing to do was return to testing and tracking.

And that's what we did. It took time. There was opposition. But eventually, we passed No Child Left Behind, which changed the federal role in education from one of ensuring equity to one of rewards and punishment all based on a new generation of flawed and biased standardized testing.

It was a brave new world where all the evils of the past were revisited on our children. And it succeeded – and continues to succeed – because we don't remember our history. We let policymakers rename the errors of our progenitors and never question their true purpose.

Both Republicans and Democrats have been in control. Both sides blame the other, but left and right wing are both complicit in what remains our national policy.

It is just as racist as that perpetrated by the eugenicists. The major difference is emphasis. In the 1920s, Terman would talk candidly about the racial order. Today, no one mentions it – not openly.

Instead, we get talk about the "racial proficiency gap." Undeniably poor minority students don't score as well on standardized tests. Instead of wondering if the problem is the assessments themselves, we're pushed to question what teachers and schools are doing wrong.

We wonder why schools serving impoverished students – who are disproportionately brown and black – apparently don't teach kids as well as schools serving wealthier populations. And anyone who mentions the difference in resources between these schools is quickly silenced. Anyone who mentions the impact of an impoverished upbringing and environment is quickly escorted from the room.

Instead of doing anything to actually help these students, our policy is to close their schools and/or turn them into fly-by-night charter schools.

"We've been able to do things – for example, close schools for academic failure. It is hugely difficult, it's hugely controversial and it's absolutely the right thing to do," said former U.S. Education Secretary Arne Duncan.[82]

Imagine if instead of "academic failure" he had said "racial and economic failure." Because that is what it comes down to. Duncan was decrying low test scores. That's why these schools were closed. But the test scores aren't the root cause. It's poverty. And it disproportionately affects minority students. But you can only see that if you admit the tests are inaccurate assessments of students' abilities – as countless peer-reviewed academic studies continue to prove.[83]

"I think the best thing that happened to the education system in New Orleans was Hurricane Katrina," Duncan famously said.[84]

The highest education official in our country actually praised a natural disaster that killed between 1,200 and 1,800 people – mostly minorities – and destroyed their public schools so they could be rebuilt as charters. Did it actually improve children's academic outcomes? No.[85]

This whole charter school push is another element of our modern educational pseudoscience. These types of schools have never been proven to help kids learn. In fact, the research shows they either do no better or often much worse[86] than traditional public schools. It is an article of faith with our modern education policymakers that schools serving poor minority children should be run by private corporations, while schools serving wealthy white students can be allowed to be run by the community.

None of this could happen without the false objectivity of standardized testing.

A hundred years ago, the eugenicists used their test scores to explain away a racist and classist social order. Today we use similarly flawed test scores to justify a similarly prejudicial social order.

Testing remains a way of keeping you in your place.

People are starting to notice. Hence the quick move by the testing industry to co-opt the largest and most well-funded civil rights organizations. Hence the Obama administration's appointing John King to succeed Duncan as U.S. Secretary of

Education – a brown face to silence racial complaints.

Are the people championing standardization and privatization racist? Honestly, I don't know. I can't see into their hearts. But it is undeniable that the results of their policies disproportionately hurt our black and brown children. Judging by their effect – not necessarily their intention – they are racist as well as classist.

Some may be true believers who actually think these policies will help children learn. I'm sure many of the eugenicists of the past felt the same way. Keeping "racially inferior" children in the slow class was purported to be for their own benefit, just as closing poor black schools today is believed to help them learn.

It is essential that we understand the terrors and errors of past education policy.

If we hadn't forgotten this dark page of American history, perhaps our children wouldn't be forced to repeat it.

STANDARDIZED TESTING CREATES CAPTIVE MARKETS

It's easy to do business when the customer is forced to buy.

But is it fair, is it just, or does it create a situation where people are coerced into purchases they wouldn't make if they had a say in the matter?

For example, school children as young as 8-years-old are forced to take a battery of standardized tests in public schools. Would educators prescribe such assessments if it were up to them? Would parents demand children be treated this way if they were consulted? Or is this just a corporate scam perpetrated by our government for the sole benefit of a particular industry that funnels a portion of the profits to our lawmakers as political donations?

Let's look at it economically.

Say you sold widgets – you know, those hypothetical doo-dads we use whenever we want to talk about selling something without importing the emotional baggage of a particular product.

You sell widgets. The best widgets. Grade A, primo, first class widgets.

Your goal in life is to sell the most widgets possible and thus generate the highest profit.

Unfortunately, the demand for widgets is fixed. Whatever they are, people only want so many of them. But if you could increase the demand and thus expand the market, you would likewise boost your profits and better meet your goals.

There are many ways you could do this. You could advertise and try to convince consumers that they need more widgets. You could encourage doctors and world health organizations to prescribe widgets as part of a healthy lifestyle. Or you could convince the government to mandate the market.

That's right – force people to buy your products.

That doesn't sound very American does it?

In a Democratic society, we generally don't want the government telling us what to purchase. Recall the hysteria around the Obamacare individual mandate requiring people who could afford to buy healthcare coverage to do so or else face a financial tax penalty? In this case, one might argue that it was justified because everyone wants healthcare. No one wants to let themselves die from a preventable disease or allow free riders to bump up the cost for everyone else.

However, it's still a captive market though perhaps an innocuous one. Most are far more pernicious.

According to dictionary.com, a captive market is "a group of consumers who are obliged ... to buy a particular product, thus giving the supplier a monopoly" or oligopoly. This could be because of lack of competition, shortages, or other factors.

In the case of government mandating consumers to buy a particular product, it's perhaps the strongest case of a captive market. Consumers have no choice but to comply and thus have little to no protection from abuse. They are at the mercy of the supplier.

It's a terrible position to be in for consumers, but a powerful one for businesspeople. And this is exactly the situation for public schools and the standardized testing industry.

Let's break it down.

These huge corporations don't sell widgets, they sell tests. In fact, they sell more than just tests, but let's focus right now on just the multiple choice, fill-in-the-bubble assessments.

Why do our public schools give these tests? Because peer-reviewed research shows they fairly and accurately demonstrate student learning? Because they've been proven by independent observers to be an invaluable part of the learning process and help students continue to learn new things?

No and no.

The reason public schools give these tests is because the government forces them. The Elementary and Secondary Education Act (ESEA) requires that all students in grades 3-8 and once in high school take certain approved standardized assessments. Parents are allowed to refuse the tests for their children, but otherwise they have to take them.

It wasn't always this way. When the act was first passed in 1965, it focused almost entirely on providing students with equitable resources. That all changed in 2001 with the passage of No Child Left Behind, a reauthorization of the original ESEA bill. And ever since, through every subsequent reauthorization and name change, the federal law governing K-12 schools has required the same standardized testing.

The testing corporations don't have to prove their products. Those products are required by law.

It's one of the largest captive markets in existence, with some 50.4 million children forced to take standardized assessments.[87] The largest such corporation, Pearson, boasts profits of $9 billion annually. Its largest competitor, CBT/ McGraw-Hill, makes $2 billion annually. Others include Education Testing Services and Riverside Publishing, better known through its parent company Houghton Mifflin Harcourt.

If many of these companies sound like book publishers, that's because they or their parent companies are. And that's no coincidence. It's another way they bolster their own market.

Not only do many of these testing corporations make, provide and score standardized assessments, they make and provide the remedial resources used to help students pass.

So if your students are having difficulty passing the state test, often the same company has a series of workbooks or a software package to help remediate them. It's a good business model. Cash in before kids take the test. Cash in when they take it. And if kids fail, cash in again to remediate them.

Ever wonder why our test scores are so low? Because it's profitable! The money is all on the side of failure, not success. In fact, from an economic point of view, there is a disincentive to succeed. Not for teachers and students, but for the people who make and grade the tests.

But that's not all.

Once you have a system in place, things can become static. Once districts already have the books and resources to pass the tests, the testing corporation has less to sell them, the market stagnates and thus their profits go down or at least stop growing.

The solution once again is to create yet another captive market. That's why Common Core was created.

These are new academic standards written almost exclusively by the testing corporations and forced on districts by federal and state governments. Under President Barack Obama's Race to the Top initiative, $500 million in federal education grants were tied to adopting these new standards. States were coerced to push Common Core on their districts or else lose out on much needed federal funding.

This resulted in the need for districts to buy all new materials – new text books, new workbooks, new software, etc. It also required the states to order brand new standardized tests. So once again the testing industry cashed in at both ends.

And these tests were more needlessly difficult so more children would fail and need costly remediation.

Was there a pressing academic need for these new standards? Was there any evidence that these standards would increase student learning? Were there even any independent studies conducted to attempt to prove a need?

No. This was a total money grab. It was naked greed from one industry completely enabled by our lawmakers at the federal and state levels.

Republicans made noises against it, and some still do. But consider this – the overwhelming majority of state houses are controlled by the GOP. They have the power to repeal Common Core at any time. Yet almost none of them did or intend to do.

Ask yourself why. It has nothing to do with the Democrats. Republicans are owned by the same masters as the so-called liberals – these same test corporations.

You have to understand that our government is no longer ruled by the principle of one person, one vote. Money has become speech, so that wealthy corporations get a huge say in what our government does.

If an industry gets big enough and makes enough donations to enough lawmakers, they get the legislation they want. In many cases, the corporations write the legislation and then tell lawmakers to pass it. And this is true for lawmakers on both sides of the aisle.

Standardized testing and Common Core are just one pernicious example of our new captive market capitalism collapsing into plutocracy.

Our tax dollars are being given away to big business and our voices of protest are silenced.

Forget selling widgets. Our children have **BECOME** widgets, hostage consumers, and access to them is being bought and sold.

We are all slaves to this new runaway capitalism that has freed itself from the burden of self-rule.

How long will we continue to put up with it?

How long will we continue to be hostages to these captive markets?

NOT MY DAUGHTER - ONE DAD'S JOURNEY TO PROTECT HIS LITTLE GIRL FROM TOXIC TESTING

I'll admit it – I was scared.

I'm a nationally board certified teacher with a master's degree in education. I've taught public school for over a dozen years. But I've only been a daddy for half that time.

Would making this call get my little girl in trouble?

I didn't want to rock the boat. I didn't want my daughter to suffer because her old man is making a fuss. I didn't want her teachers and principal giving her a hard time because of something I did or said.

But I couldn't deny what I know.

Standardized testing is destroying public education. It's stressing kids out by demanding they perform at levels they aren't developmentally ready to reach. And it's using false measures of proficiency to "prove" how bad public schools are so they can be replaced by for-profit charters that will reduce the quality of kids' educations to generate even more profits.

No. There was no doubt about it. I had to make this phone call.

I used my most professional voice on the line with the principal.

"Hi, Mr. Smith. This is Steven Singer. I'm Desi's father. I know she's just in kindergarten but it's come to my attention she's taking standardized tests, and I'd like to opt her out."

Before my little girl started school, I hadn't even realized there were standardized tests in kindergarten. She takes both the DIBELS and the GRADE test.

He seemed surprised, even a bit fearful, but he quickly suggested a meeting with me, my daughter's teacher, the counselor and a few others to get it done.

It was my turn to be surprised. I had expected to be asked to review the tests before writing a formal letter citing my "religious" reason for refusal. But I guess things are different before students reach third grade. Without legislation mandating a formal process, we needed to meet and discuss like adults.

And a few weeks later, here I was waiting for that meeting to begin.

It wasn't long before my daughter's teacher arrived. We chatted briefly about a fire drill and how my sweetheart hadn't been afraid. Then the counselor, principal and others came in and ushered us into the conference room.

Most of the space was taken up by a long rectangular table surrounded by black leather chairs on wheels. It looked like the kind of place where important decisions are made – a bit imposing really.

We sat down and Mr. Smith introduced me to the team and told them I had some concerns about standardized testing.

He paused letting me know it was my turn to speak. I took out my little notebook, swallowed and began.

"Let me start by saying I think the education my daughter is receiving here is top notch," I said.

"Her teacher is fabulous, the support staff do a wonderful job, and I could not be happier with the services she's receiving here.

"My **ONLY** concern is standardized tests. In general, I'm against them. I have no problem with teacher-created tests, just not the standardized ones.

"It's come to my attention that my daughter takes the DIBELS and GRADE test. Is that correct?"

They nodded.

"As you know, I teach at the secondary level and proctor the GRADE test to my own students. I'm sure the version given to elementary children is somewhat different, but I know first-hand how flawed this assessment is.

"Put simply, it's not a good test. It doesn't assess academic learning. It has no research behind it to prove its effectiveness, and it's a huge waste of time where kids could be learning."

I paused to see them all nodding in agreement.

In many ways, the GRADE is your typical standardized test – vocabulary, sentence completion, passage comprehension – fill-in-the-bubble nonsense.

Mr. Smith blushed in agreement. He admitted that he probably shouldn't be so candid but the district probably wouldn't give the GRADE test if it didn't receive a Keystone to Opportunity Grant for doing so. When and if the grant runs out, the district probably would stop giving the test, he said.

It's an old story – the same as at my own district. Two school systems serving high poverty populations bribed with extra money if they spend a large chunk of it on Pearson testing and remediation.

"As to the DIBELS," I went on, "I had to really do some research. As something that's only given at the elementary level, it's not something I knew much about.

"However, after reading numerous scholarly articles on the subject,[88] I decided it wasn't good for my daughter either."

When taking the DIBELS, the teacher meets with a student one-on-one while the child reads aloud and is timed with a stopwatch. Some of the words the child is asked to read make sense. Some are just nonsense words. The test is graded by how many words the child pronounces correctly in a given time period.

"My concern is that the test doesn't assess comprehension," I said. "It rewards someone who reads quickly but not someone who understands what she's reading.

"Moreover, there is a political side to the test since it's owned by Rupert Murdoch.[89] Cut scores are being artificially raised[90] to make it look like more students are failing and thus our schools aren't doing a good job.

"Finally, focusing on pronunciation separate from comprehension narrows the curriculum and takes away time from proven strategies that actually would help my daughter become a better reader."

I closed my notebook and looked around the table.

Silence.

I thought that maybe I hadn't done enough research. I had been too quick and simple.

But the team quickly agreed with me. And when Mr. Smith saw that, I noticed his cheeks darkening.

He stuttered a few words before giving up. "I've never had a parent ask to opt out of the DIBELS before," he said.

He said the DIBELS is a piece of the data teachers use to make academic decisions about their students. Without it, how would they know if their children could read, or were hitting certain benchmarks?

"I know I teach secondary and that's different than elementary," I said, "but there is not a single standardized test that I give my kids that returns any useful information.

"I don't need a test to tell me if my students can read. I don't need a test to know if they can write or spell. I know just by interacting with them in the classroom."

The fear was still in his eyes. He turned to my daughter's teacher. "I don't mean to put you on the spot here, but what do you think? Does the DIBELS provide you with useful information?" he asked.

The look on her face was priceless. It was like someone had finally asked her a question she had been waiting years to answer.

"No," she said. "I don't need the DIBELS to know if my kids can read."

It was all downhill from there.

I agreed to revisit the situation if a problem arose, but teacher recommendation would take the place of the DIBELS in the meantime.

Conversation quickly turned to hilarious anecdotes of my

daughter's school antics. What she said to get in trouble last week. How she tries to get adults to put on her coat when she's perfectly capable of doing it herself.

I left the building feeling really good. This is the way it's supposed to be.

Before we signed up my little girl for school, I had been nervous about her attending in my home district. I wasn't sure it was good enough for her. The papers said it was a failing school. I wanted so much to ensure my baby would have the best of everything – the best I could provide.

My district may not have the most up-to-date facilities. It may not have the smallest classes. But it has a team of dedicated educators and administrators who are committed to meeting the needs of their students.

Even Mr. Smith's hesitancy is understandable. I don't blame him one bit. He probably thinks DIBELS scores make an elementary principal like him look good. Kids starting from scratch only can go up. The scores can only improve.

However, he sat down with me and heard me out. He may not have entirely agreed with me – in fact at times he looked at me like I had a third arm growing out of my forehead – but he respected my parental rights.

It wasn't until then that I realized the power parents truly have. Mr. Smith might have refused a **TEACHER** who brought up all of the concerns I had. He's their boss. He trusts his own judgment.

But I don't work for him. In fact, he works for me. And – to his credit – he knows that.

I know everyone isn't as lucky as me. Some people live in districts that aren't as receptive. But if parents rose up *en masse* and spoke out against toxic testing, it would end tomorrow.

If regular everyday Dads and Moms stood up for their children and asked questions, there would be no more Race to the Top, Common Core or annual standardized testing.

Because while teachers have years of experience, knowledge and love – parents have the power.

Imagine if we all worked together! What a world we could build for our children!

STANDARDIZED TESTS EVERY DAY - THE COMPETENCY BASED EDUCATION SCAM

IN THE NOT TOO DISTANT FUTURE:

Welcome to class, children.

Please put your hands down, and sit at your assigned seat in the computer lab.

Yes, your cubicle partitions should be firmly in place. You will be penalized if your eyes wander into your neighbors testing ... I mean learning area.

Now log on to your Pearson Competency Based Education (CBE) platform.[91]

Johnny, are you reading a book? Put that away!

Are we all logged on? Good.

Now complete your latest learning module. Some of you are on module three, others on module ten. Yes, Dara, I know you're still on module one. You'll all be happy to know each module is fully aligned with Common Core State Standards.[92] In fact, each module is named after a specific standard. Once you've mastered say Module One "Citing Textual Evidence to Determine Analysis" you will move on to the next module, say "Determining Theme or Central Idea for Analysis."

Johnny, didn't I tell you to put away that book? There is no reading in school. You're to read the passages provided by the good people at Pearson.[93] No, you won't get a whole story. Most of the passages are non-fiction. But I think there is a fun passage about a pineapple coming up in your module today. Isn't that nice?

Laquan, you haven't put on your headphones and started your module yet? You've been on module three for the past week. How can you learn at your own rate if you never progress beyond module three?

What's that? Your mother wrote me a note? Let me see that.

Huh. So she wants to know how come you never get beyond module three. You should be able to answer that question for her, yourself, Laquan. (*At least you could get that one right.*)

Laquan, tell your mother that you haven't passed the proficiency standard yet. You've taken all the remediation available on the computer program, haven't you? Yes, that fun game where you answered multiple choice questions and when you got one correct the spaceship blasts an asteroid. And then you took the daily assessment but you just haven't received a passing score yet. But don't worry. I'm sure if you continue to do the same thing again today ... eventually ... you'll get it right. It's how the state and federal government determine whether you've learned anything on a daily basis.

In ancient times, teachers like me used to make up our own assignments. We'd give you books to read ... Johnny, have you started yet? ... whole books, novels, literature. And then we'd hold class discussions, class projects, act out scenes, draw posters, relate the books to your lives, write essays. But now all that silliness is gone.

Thanks to the good people at the American Legislative Exchange Council (ALEC), the Gates Foundation, and the Foundation for Excellence in Education, the state and federal government have mandated a much more efficient way of determining student learning. Back in the day, they forced schools to give one big standardized test in Reading and Math every year. Teachers would have to scramble with test prep material to make sure all learners could pass the test, because if students didn't get passing marks, the teacher was out on her butt.

We've done away with such silliness now. Thankfully the government got rid of yearly high stakes standardized testing. What we do now is called Competency Based Education. That's what this program is called. It's kind of like high stakes standardized testing every day. So much more efficient, so much more data to use to prove you know this set of basic skills written by the testing companies with hardly any input from non-experts like classroom teachers.[94]

That's how the district became composed of 100% charter schools. No more inefficient school boards made up of community members. Today our schools are run by corporate CEOs who are experts at finding ways to cut corners and increase profits for their shareholders. And, ugh, make you learn good.

Hm. I seem to be talking too much. No one's paying me to impart any information. I'm just supposed to make sure you're all hooked up to the program and making satisfactory daily progress. Otherwise, I'll be out of a job again.

You laugh, but it's hard to get minimum wage work like

this. Since the U.S. Supreme Court made labor unions all but illegal and public schools instituted CBE programs, teachers like me could no longer demand such exorbitant salaries.[95] Now I make an honest living. Speaking of which, I may have to get out of here a few minutes early today to make it to my shift at Walmart. I'm greeter today!

And if you work hard, someday you can be, too!

CO-OPTING THE LANGUAGE OF AUTHENTIC EDUCATION - THE COMPETENCY BASED EDUCATION CUCKOO

Cuckoo!

Cuckoo!

Such is the incessant cry of the hour from one of the most popular souvenirs of the black forest of Germany – the cuckoo clock.

Time is demarcated by the chirp of an 18th century animatronic bird jumping forward, moving a wing or even opening its beak before making its distinctive cry.

However, in nature the cuckoo has a more sinister reputation.

It's one of the most common brood parasites.

Instead of investing all the time and energy necessary to

raise its own young, many varieties of cuckoo sneak their eggs into the nests of other birds. When the baby cuckoos hatch, they demand an increasing amount of their clueless foster parents' care often resulting in neglect of the birds' own children.

Parental care is co-opted. The love and affection naturally needed to raise the parent birds' own children are diverted to the cuckoo's baby. And the more the parent birds try to help the interloper's child, the less they can help their own.

Corporate education reformers must be bird lovers. Or at the very least they must enjoy antique cuckoo clocks.

In fact, one could describe the entire standardization and privatization movement as a Homo sapiens version of brood parasitism.

Profiteers co-opt authentic education practices so that they no longer help students but instead serve to enrich private corporations.

When parents, teachers and administrators unwittingly engage in corporate school reform strategies to help students learn, they end up achieving the opposite, while the testing industry and charter school operators rake in obscene profits.

But some of us have seen through the scam, and we think it's cuckoo.

We've seen this kind of bait and switch for years in the language used by oligarchs to control education policy. For instance, the defunct federal No Child Left Behind legislation had nothing to do with making sure no kids got left behind. It was about focusing obsessively on test and punish even if that meant leaving poor kids in the rear view mirror.

Likewise, the Obama administration's Race to the Top program had nothing to do with quickening the pace to academic excellence. It was about glorifying competition among students while providing them inequitable resources. Teach for America has very little to do with teaching or America. It's about underpreparing poor children with unqualified instructors and giving cover to privatization operatives. School Choice has nothing to do with giving parents educational alternatives. It's about letting privatized schools choose which students they want to admit so they can go through the motions of educating them as cheaply as possible and maximize profits for shareholders.

And on and on.

The latest such scheme to hoodwink communities out of authentic learning for their children is Competency Based Education (CBE) a term used interchangeably with Proficiency Based Education (PBE). Whatever you call it, this comes out to the same thing.

Like so many failed policy initiatives that came before, it is offered by the same group of think tank sycophants, and the name belies the truth. CBE and PBE have nothing to do with making children competent or proficient in anything except taking computer-based tests.

That's what the whole program consists of – forcing children to sit in front of computers all day at school to take unending high stakes mini-tests. And somehow this is being sold as a reduction in testing when it's exactly the opposite.[96]

This new initiative is seen by many corporate school reformers as the brave new world of education policy. The public has soundly rejected standardized tests and Common Core. So this is the corporate response, a scheme they privately call stealth assessments. Students will take high stakes tests without even knowing they are doing it. They'll be asked the same kinds of multiple-choice nonsense you'd find on state mandated standardized assessments, but programmers will make it look like a game. The results will still be used to label schools "failing", regardless of how under-resourced they are or how students are suffering from the effects of poverty. Mountains of data will still be collected on your children and sold to commercial interests to better market their products.

The only difference is that they hope to trick you, to hide that it's even happening at all. And like a cuckoo pushing its egg into your nest, they hope you'll support what's in **THEIR** best interests while they work against what would really help your own children.

And the method used to achieve this deception is co-opting language. They'd never enact what real classroom teachers want in school, but they will take our language and use it to clothe their own sinister initiatives in doublespeak.

So we must pay attention to their words and tease out what they really mean.

For instance, they describe CBE as being "student-centered." And it is – in that their profit-making machine is centered on students as the means of sucking up our tax dollars.

They talk about "community partnerships," but they don't mean inviting parents and community members into the decision making process at your local school. They mean working together with your local neighborhood privatization firm to make big bucks off your child. Apple, Microsoft, Walmart – whatever huge corporation can sell computers and iPads to facilitate testing every day.

They talk about "personalized instruction," but there's nothing personal in it. CBE just means not allowing students to progress on their computer programs until they have achieved "mastery" of terrible Common Core standards. If standardized testing is a poor form of assessment, these edu-programs are worse. They don't measure understanding. They measure zombie cognitive processes – the most basic surface type of spit-it-back to me answers.

And if that isn't bad enough, such an approach subtly suggests to kids that learning is only valuable extrinsically. We don't learn for intrinsic reasons like curiosity. We lean to get badges on the program, to progress forward in the game, and to compulsively collect things – like any good consumer should.

Today's children already have problems socializing.[97] They can more easily navigate cyber relationships than real flesh-and-blood interactions. And CBE will only make this worse. Not only will children continue to spend hours of after-school time on-line, the majority of their school day will be spent seated at computer terminals, isolated from each other, eyes focused on screens. And every second they'll be monitored by that machine[98] – their keystrokes, even the direction their eyes are looking!

I'm not making this up! It shows engagement, tenacity, rigor – all measurable, quantifiable and useful to justify punishing your school. [99]

They call it "one-to-one computer technology." Yes, each child will be hooked up to one device. But how does that alone help them learn? If every child had a book, would we call it one-to-one book access? They call it "blended learning" because it mixes instruction from a living, breathing person with sit-and-stare computer time. It sounds like a recipe. I'll blend the sugar and milk until I have a nice whipped cream. But it conceals how much time is spent on each.

Don't get me wrong. There are effective uses of technology in schools. But this is not one of them.

Students can make Keynote presentations, record movies,

design graphics, write programs, etc. But taking endless testing disguised as a video game adds nothing but boredom to their day. A few years ago, I was forced by administrators to put my own students on iStation twice a week. (I've since convinced them to let us be.) In any case, when we used the program, it would have been more effective had we called it nap time. At least then my kids wouldn't have felt guilty about sleeping through it.

The corporate education reformers are trying to sneak all of this under our noses. They don't want us to notice. And they want to make it harder to actually oppose them by stealing our words.

When public school advocates demand individualized learning for their children, the testocracy offers us this sinister CBE project. When we decry annual testing, they offer us stealth assessment instead.

We must continue to advocate for learning practices that work. We can't let them steal our language, because if we do, they'll steal our ability to engage children in authentic learning.

And to do that, we must understand the con artists tricks. We have to deny the technocrats their secrecy, deny them access to our children as sources of profit.

We must guard our nests like watchful mama birds.

The cuckoos are out there.

They are chirping in the darkness all around us.

Don't let them in.

CLOSE READING - MYOPIA AS A VIRTUE

You are reading a text.

Yes. Right now.

Your eyes are scanning over symbols called letters. They are joined together into words and sentences and paragraphs and chapters to make up the totality of this book.

Your brain is in the process of translating these symbols into sounds, meanings, concepts. And you are reacting to those concepts.

You're having thoughts about what you're reading. Maybe you're reminded of a similar book or article you've read some-time in the past. Maybe you're feeling a thrill of excitement at such an original introduction to an education article. Or perhaps you're rolling your eyes and wondering why the author is such a doofus.

No matter how you look at it, reading involves complex processes. A whole bunch of stuff is going on to make it happen

– all of it essential.

Yet when we evaluate reading comprehension these days, we put the focus squarely on one or two of those multifarious processes. It's reductive, reactionary, and lame. It's a dumbing down of the cognitive and metacognitive process. But it makes things easy to grade on a standardized test.

That's what the fad of close reading[100] is all about. It's an attempt to make the mysterious and complex mind something that can easily be labeled right or wrong.[101]

For the uninitiated, close reading is the careful, sustained interpretation of a brief passage of text in which great emphasis is put on individual words, syntax, and the order in which sentences and ideas unfold.

It's not that close reading is unimportant. After all, it's something good readers do. But an overemphasis on this aspect leaves out so much that is even more vital. It's like saying the only significant part of the Hershey bar is the wrapper, or the only salient part of eating the Hershey bar is chewing. However, when I unwrap my dessert, there'd better be chocolate inside, and after I bite into it, I'd better not forget to swallow!

But education specialists with little to no actual classroom experience are making a killing going from school-to-school and lecturing teachers about how to teach.[102] And they're telling us to emphasize close reading to the detriment of everything else.

They're saying we need to give our students short texts of no more than a page or two. We should have our students read these texts without any background information about who wrote them or why.[103] We should then have students answer questions that require them to go back to the text, find something and spit it back to us.

For instance:

How does the author use figurative language to develop theme?

Explain how word choice in the passage develops characterization.

Provide examples from the passage that demonstrate the author's bias.

To the uninitiated, it looks like really important work. It's not. This is the literary equivalent of taking out the garbage or going on a scavenger hunt. These are good things, but they are not the be-all-end-all. They don't capture the essential reason we read – which is to understand.

Imagine if I asked you to go back into the part of this article you've already read and find one example of a North American pejorative used by the author. You could do it. You could scan back to the beginning, look through everything I wrote and find that I used the word "Doofus."

Huzzah! You win the scavenger hunt.

Now explain why I used that word by making reference to textual evidence. You could do that, too. You could look at all the other things I've written so far and explain why I probably chose that word.

Congrats!

But notice what you can't do, what these think tank clones will never ask you to do – *form a substantial opinion*. Not just why do you think someone else did something, but what do you think about what they did?

For example:

Do you think the use of colloquialisms and slang have a place in serious education theory? Why or why not?

When was the most or least effective time you or a colleague used a colloquialism to express a complex thought? Evaluate its effectiveness.

In what ways are forbidden words more or less meaningful than those more easily sanctioned?

At its core, reading is not about discrete facts. No one picks up a piece of text to find minute fragments of information. Instead, we're looking for enlightenment. We don't care so much about how the astronaut puts on the spacesuit. We want to know why she put it on in the first place. We want to know where she's going. We want to know what it's like and if we'd want to do something like that ourselves.

But an overemphasis on close reading ignores all this. It pretends readers are robots. It pretends reading is a mechanical process that can be easily divided into its component parts and examined discretely.

Even worse it ignores the needs of individual students. For many children in our modern world, reading of this sort is almost entirely alien to their lives. There are so many things competing for our attention these days that reading often gets neglected. Even if you love to read, it can be difficult to find the time and inclination to sit down, quiet yourself, and just read.

THIS is where most educators would like to focus – getting students to read at all. We want to show learners why they might want to read. We want to engage them. Demonstrate what an amazing experience a good book can be. We want to foster that look of delight in their eyes, that sense of wonder, the epiphany of literacy.

But instead we're being told to focus on the nuts and bolts, the everyday boring hunt and seek of mechanical mentation.

Whatever you do, don't see the forest – see the individual

trees. Don't look at the big picture, look exclusively to the details and don't worry your pretty little head about making any larger meaning out of it.

This is tantamount to child abuse. We're putting blinders on children's minds and telling them which direction to think. We're taking away their ownership of the reading experience. It's no longer about what they want, what they've lived through, what they believe or what they see. It's only about the author's view – an author they probably don't care about because they had no part in all the other crucial facets of the reading experience. In fact, I would argue that this isn't even really reading at all. It's little more than decoding. It's a skill set fit for a corporate drone, not someone in management or any position to make valuable decisions.

It's no wonder that these prescriptions are only leveled at public schools. Parochial, private and charter schools are specifically left out of these mandates. The same people demanding close reading for your kids want something much different for their own.[104]

This is class warfare as education policy. It's all about keeping down working families and lifting up the one percent.

That's essentially what corporate education reform is all about – every tentacle of the beast is wrapped around the young minds of the poor, the brown skinned, the undesirable.

But perhaps you don't agree with me. Perhaps you have your own thoughts on this matter which may differ from mine.

Fine, I say. Good!

Yes, please think about it. Ponder these issues carefully, because while I'm championing free thought, the other side wants nothing less than your children's complete submission to the *status quo*.

Feel free to give that a nice close read.

WHY IS COMMON CORE STILL HERE?

Common Core has become a national joke.

In fact, the set of academic standards has inspired a new genre of grade school humor – Common Core comedy.

For instance:

One student turns to another and says, "Common Core is about making us college and career ready."

The other student replies, "It's working. It's making me drink more every day."

Here's another one:

Question: Why can't mommy help you with your Common Core math homework?

Answer: She only has a four-year degree.

And finally:

Question: How many whiteboards does it take to show you how to screw in a light bulb?

Answer: One, but it takes dozens to explain 1+4 in Common Core.

Parents nationwide know the pain of Common Core[105] by the looks on their children's faces.

They see bright, curious youngsters go to school and come back hating math education[106] and thinking they're stupid.

Parents get the same feeling trying to decipher their children's homework.

Meanwhile the majority of teachers hate the standards – and as they become more familiar with Common Core, that number grows every year.

So why do we keep using Common Core? Why haven't our schools thrown this bad idea on the trash heap of failed education policies?

In short – because industry is making a lot of money from it.[107]

Common Core was created by private corporations.[108]

It was not made by the states,[109] nor was it written by the federal government.

It was created to sell a new generation of standardized tests and textbooks.[110]

Its *raison d'etre* is not education, it's profit.

Before its inception, school children didn't need a unified set of academic standards. Big business needed them to sell more books and tests.

The standards were written by Achieve, Inc.[111], a Washington, D.C., organization formed in 1996 by corporate leaders and six state governors. The endeavor was funded by Bill Gates and other business interests. It was reviewed by individuals and organizations also funded by Gates.

Then the federal government stepped in to strongly encourage states to adopt the standards. Not because anyone actually thought they were necessary. They did it because that was what wealthy donors wanted.

Eventually the standards were adopted in 42 states, but not because legislatures voted on them. The standards were quietly approved[112] by state boards of education, unelected state education chiefs, and boards of education. Many lawmakers didn't even know what Common Core was or that their state had implemented it until voters started calling and asking questions.

Moreover, at the time of their adoption, the standards weren't even completed. They were enacted in many cases sight unseen.

How did the federal government get state officials to do this? Money and threats.[113]

Public schools were strapped because of the great recession. So the Barack Obama administration swooped in to help – on the condition that states enact a series of reforms including Common Core.

The Obama administration did not write Common Core, but it did everything it could to make sure states enacted these standards. In the 2009 stimulus package, there was $4.35 billion in discretionary funds given to the U.S. Department of Education to hand out as state grants. But in order to qualify for these grants, states had to adopt the Common Core. With education funding at a premium, bureaucrats were only too willing to bend over backwards to keep their state's schools running.

And when the carrot wasn't enough, the federal government used the stick.

Many states were applying to the federal government for waivers to the disastrous No Child Left Behind legislation. Adopting Common Core and several other corporate education reforms was made a pre-condition. If states didn't adopt these standards, their schools would be labeled "failing" and lose even more federal funding.

Despite all this, the media still often misrepresents the facts.[114]

It is objectively verifiable that the Common Core was written by private industry. So the media never asks that question. It asks if the Common Core was "state-led." That way there is room for spin.

Who led the effort to enact these standards? Since a handful of governors and other government officials were involved in their creation, media patsies are able to pretend the initiative started with the states. But don't believe it. It started with private interests – people like David Coleman and Bill Gates[115] – trying to influence government to do what they wanted for their own ends. As President of the College Board, Coleman stood to profit off new books and tests. As co-founder of Microsoft, Gates stood to profit from the new technology needed to run many of these new tests and materials. They led the initiative, not the states.

No government official was ever given a mandate by the voters or their empowered representatives to create or enact Common Core. Those that did so acted in their private capacities. Bribing a handful of governors doesn't make something a state initiative.

Just because a government official does something doesn't make it policy. When Chris Christie orders a foot long hoagie for lunch, it isn't the start of a government program to feed people at Subway. He's just ordering lunch.

Moreover, when government officials are coerced into adopting a policy because otherwise they won't be able to fulfill their obligations to voters, that isn't an endorsement of those policies. You can't offer a starving child a sandwich on the condition that he shouts a swear word and then pretend it was all his idea. You can't offer a glass of water to a man dying of thirst on the condition that he shave his head and then pretend that he likes being bald.

Common Core was not adopted by states because they liked it. It was adopted to keep schools running.

Special interests used the federal government's power over the states to circumvent the legislative process.

The result is a set of poor quality standards[116] that are developmentally inappropriate and don't help students learn. This should be no surprise since they were written with minimal input from classroom teachers, child psychologists, colleges of education, education specialists, or anyone knowledgeable about children's learning.. Instead they were created by standardized test authors. But even if the standards had been good, the process of their adoption was highly undemocratic.

Sadly, this is how government works now.

Charter schools, Teach for America, standardized testing – public education has been high jacked by business interests.

Once upon a time, the goal was to help students learn. Now the main objective is to help big business profit off students.

If you can make a buck off something – even if it doesn't help or actually hurts school kids – do it.

Nowhere is this clearer than with the Common Core.

Unfortunately, neither Democrats nor Republicans seem to get it.

Both parties misunderstand the problems with Common Core.

Democrats most often think the only issue is the way the Common Core was implemented in schools – not federal coercion, not poor quality standards, etc. In actuality, schools didn't implement them too quickly. The standards are badly written, unproven to help and increasingly shown to hurt.

President Donald Trump and the Republicans, on the other hand, think it's all wrong, but they have no idea what to do about it. They act as if the only problem with the standards is Obama's participation. They conveniently ignore or omit the past advocacy of prominent members of their own party like Jeb Bush, Chris Christie, Bobby Jindal, and Mike Huckabee.

Neither side seems to understand that the federal government can't really do much about the Common Core one way or another. The new federal education law, the Every Student Succeeds Act (ESSA) bans the federal government from doing anything to promote Common Core, or any other set of education standards. Despite all Trump's blather to the contrary, the federal government does not have the power to repeal the standards, just as it didn't have the power to enact them in the first place. So it falls to the states to step up and take action.

Each state legislature can keep, revise, or repeal Common Core. And in some cases, this has already begun. In Oklahoma, for example, Common Core was repealed entirely. In other states, like New Jersey, Common Core has been revised but largely left in place. In other states, the standards remain untouched.

So why hasn't Common Core gone away? State legislatures haven't acted.

If Common Core is eventually repealed – and that's what

the majority of taxpayers want[117] – we can only hope it's done so in a more democratic fashion than when it was approved. And we can only hope it isn't replaced with something worse.

Whatever happens, it should be to benefit students, not corporations.

Or to put it another way:

Question: What if Common Core was created just to drive parents crazy?

Answer: Somebody must be making a fortune on crazy meds!!

NATIONAL ACADEMIC STANDARDS - TURNING PUBLIC EDUCATION INTO MCSCHOOLS

America is obsessed with standardization.

Let's make everything the same – neat and uniform.

It's ironic coming from a country that's always been so proud of its rugged individualism.

But look almost anywhere in the U.S. of A, and you'll see a strip mall with almost all of the same stores and fast food restaurants selling the same crusty burgers and fries left waiting for the consumer under a heat lamp.

Somehow this has become **THE** model for public education, as well. Corporations have convinced our lawmakers that the disposable franchise business schematic is perfect to increase student learning.

That's where we got the idea for Common Core. All schools should teach the same things at the same times in the same ways.

It's been a horrendous failure.

But this chapter isn't about the Common Core *per se*. It isn't about how the Common Core is unpopular, expensive, developmentally inappropriate, created by non-experts, or illegal. It's about the very idea of national academic standards. After all, if the Common Core is flawed, one might suggest we simply fix those flaws and institute a better set of national standards. I contend that this would be a failure, too.

The problem with standardization is that it forces us to make uniform choices. In situation A, we always do **THIS**. In Situation B, we always do **THAT**. There are some areas where this is a good thing, but education is not one of them.

For instance, we can all agree that children need to read books, but what kind of books? Should they read mostly fiction or nonfiction? Should books be limited by subjects or should they be chosen by interest? Should they be ebooks or hardcopies? Should they be organized by grade level or an individual's reading level?

These are decisions that are best made in class by the teacher. However, when we write national standards, we're taking away educators' autonomy and giving it to some nameless government entity. This isn't smart. Teachers are the scientists of the classroom. They can use their observational skills to determine what a child needs and how best to meet those needs. If we remove this, we're forced to guess what hypothetical children will need in hypothetical situations. Even under the best of circumstances, guesses will not be as good as teacher's informed judgement.

But, some will say, standards should be broad. They shouldn't determine what children will learn in detail. They just set a framework. For instance, they'll detail that all children should learn how to add and subtract. All children will learn how to read and write.

There is some truth to this. We can all agree to a basic framework of skills children need before graduation. However, if the framework is this broad, is it even necessary?

Do you really think there are any public schools in this country that don't attempt to teach mathematics? Are there any schools that don't teach reading and writing?

I doubt such educational institutions exist, and even if they did, you wouldn't need national academic standards to change them. By any definition, they would be cheating their students. If the community found out this was going on, voters would make sure things changed.

What about evolution, someone asks. This is a central scientific concept vital to a modern understanding of the field that in many places isn't being taught in our public schools. Don't we need national standards to ensure things like evolution are part of the curriculum?

The short answer is no.

For a moment, let me remove my ban on talking about Common Core – our current attempt at national standards. Some people defend it with this same argument. However, it should be noted that the Common Core has no science and history standards. It does nothing to ensure evolution is taught in schools.

But could we ever have standards that did ensure evolution is taught? Yes, we could.

Why don't we? Why doesn't Common Core explicitly address this? Because enacting such standards would take political power of a sort that doesn't exist in this country. Too many voters oppose it. No state or federal legislature would be able to pass it.

But let's assume for a moment that the political stars had

aligned, and we could get lawmakers to vote for this. Why would they need to? This is a central theory of so many fields of science. Do we need an act of Congress to make sure all schools teach about gravity? Do we need one for nuclear forces? Friction?

You don't need a Congressional order to teach science. If the community wants it, teachers will just do it. That's their job. You can't legislate that everyone believes in evolution. You have to convince people that it should be taught. National standards won't change that. You can't sneak it in under Newton's laws of motion. We need to come to consensus as a society. As much as I truly believe evolution should be taught in schools, national standards are not going to make that happen.

Even if I were wrong, the cost would be far too high. We shouldn't want all of our public schools to be uniform. When everyone teaches the same things, it means we also leave out the same things. There is far too much to know in this world than can ever be taught or learned in one lifetime. Choices will always need to be made. The question is who should make them?

If we allow individuals to make different choices, it diversifies what people will know. Individuals will make decisions, which will become the impetus to learning, which will then become intrinsic and therefore valued. Then when you get ten people together from various parts of the country, they will each know different things but as a whole they will know so much more than any one member of the group. If they all know the same things, as a group they are no stronger, no smarter than each separate individual. That is not good for society.

We certainly don't want this ideal when going out to eat. We don't want every restaurant to be the same. We certainly don't want every restaurant to be McDonalds.

Imagine if every eatery was a burger joint. That means there would be no ethnic food. No Mexican. No Chinese. No Italian. There would be nothing that isn't on that one limited menu. Moreover, it would all be prepared the same way. Fast food restaurants excel in consistency. A Big Mac at one McDonalds is much like a Big Mac at any other. This may be comforting but – in the long run – it would drive us insane. If our only choices to eat were on a McDonald's Value Menu, we would all soon die of diabetes.

But this is what we seem to want of our public schools. Or do we? There is a bait and switch going on in this argument for school standardization. When we talk about making all schools the same, we're not talking about all schools. We're only talking about traditional public schools. We're not talking about charter schools, parochial schools or private schools.

How strange! The same people who champion this approach rarely send their own children to public schools. They want sameness for your children but something much different for their own.

I have never heard anyone say this approach should be applied to all schools across the board. That's very telling. These folks want your kids to be limited to the McDonald's Value Menu while their kids get to go to a variety of fancy restaurants and choose from a much daintier display.

If standardization were so great, why wouldn't they want it for their own children? I think that proves how disingenuous this whole argument is. Standardization makes no one smarter. It only increases the differences between social classes.

Rich children will get a diverse individualized education while poor children get the educational equivalent of a Happy Meal.

Think about it. Every generation of American that has ever gone to public school managed to get an excellent education without the need for national academic standards. Steve Jobs, Jeff Bezos, Bill Clinton, Ronald Reagan, Carl Sagan, Ruth Bader Ginsberg, Spike Lee, Larry King, and Stan Lee along with 90% of the United States population went to public school. None of them needed national academic standards to succeed.

This is a solution in search of a problem. The only reason we're being sold the need for these standards is because it makes it easier for corporations to profit off federal, state and local tax dollars set aside for education. New standards mean new text books, new tests, new test prep materials, new software, and new computers. In the case of Common Core, it also means failing as many children as possible to secure a never ending demand for all of these things and an open door to privatization.

We must wake up to the lies inherent in these sorts of policies. Yes, the Common Core is horrible, but the problem goes far beyond the Common Core.

National Academic Standards are a terrible idea propagated by the 1% to turn the rest of us into barely educated sub-humans and boost the corporate bottom line.

Do you want fries with that?

PART IV

TEACHING

PUTTING THE ARTS BACK IN LANGUAGE ARTS - ONE JOURNAL AT A TIME

Sometimes in public school you've just got to cut the crap.

No testing. No close reading. No multiple choice nonsense.

Get back to basics – pass out notebooks, crack them open and students just write.

Not an essay. Not a formal narrative. Not an official document. Just pick up a pencil and see where your imagination takes you.

You'd be surprised the places you'll go.

You might invent a new superhero and describe her adventures in a marshmallow wonderland. You might create a television show about strangers trapped in an elevator. You might imagine what life would be like if you were no bigger than a flea.

Or you might write about things closer to home. You might

describe what it's like to have to take care of your three younger brothers and sisters after school until just before bedtime when your mom comes back from her third minimum wage job. You might chronicle the dangers of walking home after school dismissal where drug dealers rule certain corners and gangs patrol the alleys. You might report on where you got those black and blue marks on your arms, your shoulders, places no one can see when you're fully clothed.

My class is not for the academic all stars. It's for children from impoverished families, kids with mostly black and brown skin, and test scores that threaten to close their school and put me out of work.

So all these topics and more are fair game. You can write about pretty much whatever you want. I might give you something to get you started. I might ask you a question to get you thinking, or try to challenge you to write about something you've never thought about or to avoid certain words or phrases that are just too darn obvious. I might ask your opinion of something in the news or what you think about the school dress code or get your thoughts about how things could improve.

Because I actually care what you think.

Strange, I know.

At times like these, I'm not asking you to dig through a nonfiction text or try to interpret a famous literary icon's grasp of figurative language. It's not the author's opinion that matters – it's yours – because you are the author. Yes, **YOU**.

You matter. Your thoughts matter. Your feelings. **YOU MATTER!**

And sometimes students raise their hands and ask me to read what they've written. And sometimes – more often than not – the first thing they say is, "It's no good." "I don't like it."

"I did bad on this."

So I stop reading, I look them right in the eyes and ask them who wrote it.

"Me?" they say.

And I respond, "Then I'm sure it's excellent." And it usually is.

My 8th grade students have been ground down so low under the weight of a society that couldn't care less about their well-being that they've begun to internalize it. They think their thoughts and feelings are worthless. No one cares about what they think.

But I do.

So I offer them a chance to share what they've written. I don't demand. I don't force anyone to read anything. I know that some things that spill out on the page aren't for sharing. But I want them to know that I value what they've just put down and that I think it's worth taking the class time to let others hear it, too.

"Mr. Singer, I wrote five pages," Jaquae tells me this afternoon. "That's too long to share."

"I disagree," I say. "If you think it's worth our time, you should read it. You deserve our attention."

So he reads, blows out a cleansing breath, and smiles.

In the process, we all become ennobled. We become more. We become a community. We get a peek at our common humanity.

It's so easy to look at others as mere adversaries. Even our national education policy sees things in terms of a competition, a race. We set children against each other for points, for grades, for attention, just to feel valuable. *You're a Proficient.*

You're a Basic. You're a Below Basic. And somewhere along the way children lose the sense that they're all valuable, because they're all human beings with thoughts, feelings and experiences that no one else has ever gone through before – but to which everyone can relate.

So I write, too. Every time I set my students a journal, I put pen to paper, as well.

At the beginning of the year, I share what I wrote to show them that it's okay. At the middle of the year I ask them if they want me to share. And at the end of the year I remain silent unless they ask me to do otherwise.

Because these class moments aren't about me. They're about them. I'm willing to be as much a part of their creative space as they want, but it's a choice, not a dictate.

In my class I will make you learn, but I don't control *what* you learn or *how* you feel about it.

I extend my students this respect because I know that what we're really doing isn't some meaningless exercise. We're creating art.

Not just scribbles on a page. Not something done just to please the teacher. This is an excavation of the soul. We dive into the depths of ourselves and come back all the better for it.

That's why my students write in a journal almost every day.

That's why we put mechanics and spelling and grammar aside for a few moments and just write what we need to say.

Because Language Arts, after all, is an Art. It says that right in the title.

My students are artists. Often, I am their muse. I hold a mirror up to their fractured and beaten spirits to show them the grandeur of what resides inside them.

And hopefully they come away inspired.

Because they are wonders. They are joyous. They are little pieces of my heart.

NOTE: This chapter was published as the fifth in a series of blog posts by various authors focused on the value of art in our lives, and the role art can play in resisting the test and punish model of education.[118]

FORGET CORPORATIONS - UNIONS REALLY ARE PEOPLE

One word.

That's all it takes to make some folks explode with anger.

One **PARTICULAR** word.

Not the F-word.

Or the C-word.

Or even the N-word.

It's the U-word. **UNIONS!**

Say that word, especially in a positive light, and heads burst like rotten pumpkins holding freshly lit firecrackers!

Eyes narrow, nostrils flare, a vein pops out on a forehead – and then a diatribe comes pouring out of your interlocutor's mouth like the deep-seated, half-digested bile it is.

I just don't get it.

Unions are people, after all.

Mitt Romney may have earned himself a place in the Presidential Candidate Hall of Shame for saying the same of corporations. But where he was wrong about the company, firm or business – it's more truthful to speak this way of labor unions. Or any Democratic institution, for that matter.

No, I don't mean that unions are individual entities that have lives of their own and deserve civil rights. But the people who make up those unions do.

That's the whole point. Unions are made up of people. Their whole purpose is to fight for the rights of the individuals in them.

Corporations, on the other hand, have people who work for them, yes, but their *raison d'etre* is to earn profits for the executives, the board of directors and shareholders only.

While both work for the good of their members, unions work for **ALL** of their members. Corporations only work for the good of a limited selection of those connected with them – the owners.

At least that's how it's supposed to work. There are unions that work well and those that don't. But the concept of a labor union – all the workers at a place of business gathering together to equal the power of the owners – is a good one.

Critics, however, see everything about unions as wrong.

They accuse unions of (1) stifling flexibility and creativity in the workplace. They say unions are (2) Communist, (3) politically allied to the Democrats and (4) increase costs. Among other things.

Let's examine these claims.

1) Unions stifle flexibility and creativity

Naysayers act as if unions impose rules on the helpless

bosses. This is untrue. There is nothing in any union contract that was not agreed on by both parties. Sometimes it's quite difficult to reach agreement. Often compromises are made on both sides. But each party has an equal say in what goes into the agreement.

As a result, sometimes the contract gets in the way of an easy fix to a problem. But is that really surprising for a document born of compromise? Neither party gets exactly what it wants. They meet in the middle. Sure, it would be much more flexible for the owners to make all the decisions. Likewise, it would be more flexible if the workers got to make all the decisions, too. But would either really lead to the best working environment?

Take break periods. If it were up to most managers, workers wouldn't get any time to recoup from the constant demands of the job. They'd have to keep going with no respite until quitting time – maybe with a brief working lunch.

So union contracts often require breaks in the day. Not as much as workers would like, and not as few as the bosses would prefer either. To achieve this, you lose some flexibility.

For instance, if the contract says workers get two 15-minute breaks, you can't combine them into one 30-minute breather. This makes it difficult if you're needed at your post but have to stop suddenly to punch out. Otherwise, you won't have time for both breaks.

It would seem to make more sense to keep working now and take a longer respite later. However, that is not what management and labor agreed to do.

It's a compromise to benefit both parties. Workers are assured of having breaks in their day while management is assured that labor can't take advantage of the situation by manipulating the clock to get a prolonged period off. If it becomes a problem, both parties can revisit it and make changes during the next contract negotiations. It may be difficult to change deeply embedded practices, but it can be done.

It doesn't stop anyone from being creative. It just means you have to work within certain guidelines – and doing that may actually require innovation!

2) Unions are Communist

This is patently false. In fact, there are few more democratic institutions than labor unions.

All decisions are made by majority rule. Members vote on who serves as officers, who will have a seat on the negotiation committee, whether to accept a contract, when and if to go on strike, etc. That doesn't sound like Soviet Russia! It sounds like Independence Hall in Philadelphia!

The only difference is it attempts to equalize power between the workers and the boss. It never actually achieves this ideal, but it does increase the say of the workers over the fat cats of the world.

That is not communism. It's a respect for people's individual rights.

Think about it. You don't lose your human rights the moment you take a job. Why should the owners get free reign over their employees? Likewise, owners don't lose all their power just because they need other human beings to make the goods and/or services they provide. Labor shouldn't get to dictate everything either. It's a give-and-take. When working well, it brings out the best in everyone.

Let's be clear. **THIS** is what critics are really railing against. They'd rather preserve the owner's power. The idea that the elites have to listen at all to menial workers just rubs them the wrong way. They'd rather be the ones making all the decisions – just like Pol Pot, Mao Zedong or Kim Jong-il. Come to think of it, the non-union workplace is more like Stalingrad than the union one.

Without unions, workers are at the mercy of their employers. Not exactly a red, white and blue proposition!

3) Unions are politically allied to the Democratic Party

How I wish this were true!

It would be great if one political party stood up for the rights of the working man! Unfortunately neither donkey nor pachyderm is exactly itching for the job.

Historically, the Democrats have done more to increase unions' power than the Republicans. But that's a pretty old and dusty history book you're reading.

In the past 40 years, both parties have gleefully striped away union protections and rights. The only difference is that some Democratic politicians concede the right of unions to actually exist. Many Republicans act as if they would abolish the institution at the first opportunity.

Rank and file union members vote based on the platforms of the candidates involved. If there were a Republican candidate running on pro-union policies, union members would probably vote for him. That's just called Democracy.

If a party wants the union vote, just give workers a reason to vote for your candidates.

4) Unions raise costs

Yes, and no.

In the short term, they do. But in the long run, unions may actually increase profits thereby paying for any increased initial investment.

When your business has a labor union, you have to pay higher wages. You need more safety regulations so fewer people get hurt on the job. You pay more for healthcare and pension plans. You have to cover more paid leaves and vacation times.

This is true. But it's not a liability. It's an advantage.

When you treat workers well, the quality of their work increases. It just makes sense. If people are happy at the job, they're going to do it better than those who hate it. This increases the quality of your product and, thus, sales. So you may have to pay more money upfront, but it gets offset by profits. Does the increase justify the cost? That depends.

Every business needs customers. Without money, consumers can't buy the goods and/or services you provide. So when you pay a higher salary, you're creating a potential market.

Consider this. When workers have more money, that's cash that goes right back into the economy. They have money to buy stuff, maybe even the stuff you're selling. That's why Henry Ford famously made sure to increase wages at his auto factories – so that his employees could afford to buy the very cars they were making!

5) But what about non-union workers? Is it fair that union labor gets all this while everyone else is left wanting?

The short answer – yes.

If you're jealous of the benefits of being in a union, join one. Don't tear down someone else. Don't be a resentful child popping another kid's balloon because Mommy didn't buy you one. Go get yours. Unionized labor will welcome you with open arms.

Petulant envy is exactly the attitude the bosses want you to take. You can always tell a news source is bought-and-paid-for when you hear some talking head spouting such petty, childish nonsense.

But leaving aside those who'd rather bring you down than boost themselves up, there's an even more important reason to support unions. Membership actually benefits all – even non-unionized labor!

It's called the free market. When unions boost salary and fringe benefits at one business, others have to do the same to compete. If your business doesn't pay the same high salaries, it will lose the best employees to businesses that do. That's simple economics.

None of this is seriously in contention. These are proven historical facts. Naysayers really just don't want to pay a fair wage. They'd rather pay as little as possible and thus bring down salaries and benefits across the board.

In fact, as unions have decreased, that's exactly what's happened!

It's a matter of point of view. Should we aim for a shared prosperity in this country or a limited one? Should we aspire to be a nation that's best for all or only for some? I know my answer.

6) What about the global marketplace? Don't unions make it harder for the U.S. to compete with foreign markets, especially those in the third world?

Again, the answer is both yes and no.

Sure, it costs more to treat workers as human beings rather than indentured servants. When you pay a living wage, your costs will be more and your profits initially lower than those of a company that keeps its workers in dormitories and has suicide nets outside the windows. But do we really want to compete with that? Is that the kind of America you want to live in? Does your morality really allow you to make money off of the misery of your employees?

Heck! Why pay workers at all? Slavery has a much better return on investment. The owners can keep people alive as cheaply as possible and then just work them to death. Profits would soar!

Assuming, of course, there's anyone left to buy anything! That's a pretty big problem. Right now, the third world is only able to continue these practices because it has a willing market here in the U.S. Without us buying these cheap products, they wouldn't have customers and, thus, couldn't continue.

Instead of slobbering all over ourselves in covetousness at their inhumane business practices, we should be putting political pressure on these third world companies to reform! We should boycott their products.

The irony, of course, is that many of the most egregious crimes committed against third world peoples are perpetrated by U.S. companies who've outsourced their labor. We are selling short our own workers by preferring brown and black people in foreign lands whom we can more easily exploit.

If Americans had higher wages, they could more easily disengage from these abuses! If U.S. consumers had higher salaries, they'd be more choosey about what they buy – they'd spend more freely on high quality goods – like the kind made by a unionized workforce.

In short, we need to stop shaming hard-working people from using their collective power to improve their lives. There's nothing wrong with demanding fair treatment. Human beings deserve to be treated humanely.

And that's exactly what unions are. Human beings.

They are engineers, nurses, auto-workers, letter-carriers and food service employees.

They are your teachers, police and fire fighters.

They are fathers, mothers, sisters, brothers, sons and daughters.

They're just people.

Not a dirty word.

UNIONS CAN'T JUST BE ABOUT WHAT WE'RE ALLOWED TO DO - SOCIAL JUSTICE UNIONISM

If labor unions were an animal, they'd be an old hound dog napping on the porch.

They're slow to get up and chase away burglars but they do like to howl at night.

Most of the time you don't even know they're around until the dinner bell rings. Then that ancient mutt is first to bolt into the kitchen to find a place at the table.

It's kind of sad really. That faithful old dog used to be really something in his youth.

He was fierce! He'd bark at trespassers even tearing them apart if they threatened his patch of land.

Old Uncle Sam used to yell at him and even threaten the pooch with a rolled up newspaper, but that dog didn't care. He had a sense of right and wrong, and he didn't mind getting into deep trouble fighting for what he thought was fair.

Today, however, the only thing that really riles him is if you threaten to take away his ratty old bone.

Let's face it. Unions have become kind of tame. They're housebroken and not much of a threat to those people waiting in the shadows to rob us blind.

Some people say we'd be better off without them. But I don't agree. Even a decrepit canine can act as a deterrent, and thieves sure are frightened of dogs.

Think about all unions have given us – the weekend, child labor laws, vacation time, pensions, lunch breaks, healthcare, the 8-hour day, maternity leave, safety measures, due process, sick leave and free speech protections on the job![119]

They didn't get us all that by sitting politely at the table with their hands crossed. They didn't do all that by contributing modest sums to political campaigns. They didn't do it by obsessively protecting collective bargaining at the expense of all else.

Unions used to take to the streets. They took over the job site. They marched with signs and placards. They exercised people power.

And the government was scared of them. The President called out the army to get them back to work. Lawmakers hired mercenaries to break strikes with clubs and guns. But eventually Congress passed laws to placate them.

Unfortunately, That was a long time ago.

For decades the pendulum has been swinging against unions. Federal and state laws have become increasingly restrictive. They want to tell us when we can strike and how long. They want to tell us when and if we can collect dues. And frankly, they want to tell us to just disperse and do whatever the bosses want – because the business class has already bought and paid for our politicians.

For decades we've heard their propaganda on TV, the radio and the print media. Well-paid shills have poured their poison in our ears about the evils of the labor movement. They've spoken these lies so often lots of people believe them.

Workers used to fight to make sure everyone got a fair deal. Now the working man has been brainwashed to focus instead on making sure no one else gets more than him. And the bosses are laughing all the way to the bank.

Union membership is at the lowest it's been in a century[120]. So are wages adjusted for inflation.[121] A family of four used to be able to get by comfortably on one salary. Now it can barely make ends meet with two.

Yes. There's no doubt about it. We need unions today more than ever.

But for unions to survive, they must change. They have to become a reflection of the membership and not just of the union leaders.

During the last presidential election cycle, we saw our largest national unions – the National Education Association (NEA) and the American Federation of Teachers (AFT) endorsing a candidate without bothering to actively poll their members. We saw them speak for us on policy decisions without asking our opinions. We saw them act just like the corrupt politicians who we should be fighting against.

Yes, it is time for a change. No longer can our unions be run from the top down. They must be run from the bottom up. They shouldn't tell us what to do. We, the membership, should be giving orders to them.

Moreover, we need to stop obsessing about collective bargaining. I'm not saying that's unimportant. But it can't be the only thing we do.

Our unions used to be in the midst of larger social movements. We were part of the Civil Rights movement. We were part of the push for desegragation. We were part of the fight to protect children and provide them a decent education.

We need to continue that today. And in some places we are already doing that! Look to Chicago, Detroit and Philadelphia. Teachers unions in those urban areas are fighting not just for better pay and benefits but for the communities they serve. Detroit teachers en mass are calling off work sick to protest horrible conditions in the schools. Chicago teachers are marching in the streets with the community to demand indictments for police murdering their black and brown students. Philadelphia teachers are supporting students who walk out of class to protest state disinvestment and toxic testing.

THIS is what unions should be doing. We should be fighting for social justice. We should be a central part of the struggle to turn the tide against corporatization, privatization and standardization of our country's public goods. We should be marching hand-in-hand with BlackLivesMatter activists. We should be in the front lines of the fight to save our environment and replace fossil fuels with renewable energy.

We must be *part* of the community and not *apart* from it. We must share in the struggles and goals of those we serve. We must be an example of the old truism that a rising tide raises all ships. After all, the word "union" literally means together. By definition we must all be in this together or else we're not even really a union.

And to do this we have to stop being so concerned with what they tell us we can and cannot do.

We live in a democratic society. The government gets its power from us, from our consent. That means that if there are enough of us, we trump their corrupt laws. They only get to make those laws because we say so. And court decisions – even Supreme Court decisions – mean nothing next to the court of public opinion.

The bosses buy the politicians and tell them to legislate us into a box. It's time to break out of that box. We can't be afraid to take our power back. We shouldn't be afraid of our government. Our government should be afraid of us.

How do we do it? Organize.

If you belong to a union, roll up your sleeves and get active. Run for office. Convince like-minded folks to join you. Take over your local branch. Spread to your national branch.

If you don't belong to a union, start one at your job. Talk to your co-workers. Talk about the benefits for each of you and your neighborhoods. Fight for your rights.

I know. It's a whole lot easier to complain. Real change, though, takes real work.

We used to know these things. Somewhere along the line we forgot.

So wake up, you yeller cur dog, and get off the porch. Take to the streets.

Because the surest way to take back our country is to take back our unions.

SUMMER BREAK - THE LEAST UNDERSTOOD AND MOST MALIGNED ASPECT OF A TEACHER'S LIFE

It's inevitable.

Once the weather gets warm and school lets out, it's no longer safe for teachers to be out in public.

You've got to stay indoors, get off the Internet, hide the cell phone – do whatever you can to stay away from non-educators.

Because if, like me, you happen to be out and about – let's say standing in line at your favorite neighborhood burger joint waiting for a juicy slab of ground beef to stop sizzling on the grill – you're bound to hear the kind of willful ignorance that sets a teacher's nerves permanently on edge.

Imagine just two normal people – they seem nice enough – standing in line having a friendly conversation. It's hot outside, so you might hear the usual topics discussed – the weather, the best place to buy ice cream, which public pool has the best prices, and "*oh I don't know, how easy teachers have it with their summers off.*"

Son of a …!

Normal folks, I know you often get the urge to talk about this. You think it's just another topic of polite conversation. It's nothing serious. You think it's just like complaining about the heat or how the price of admission at the local theme park always seems to be on the rise.

But you're wrong.

Here's why. First, you aren't alone in the comfort of your own home. You're out in public. And I guarantee there's probably a teacher somewhere within earshot. Second, you have no idea what the heck you're talking about. You are completely talking out of your ass.

Oh, you *think* you know. Everyone thinks they know what it's like to be a teacher. Everyone thinks they can do that job no matter what qualifications they have.

It's funny. I never presume to assume I could do other people's jobs without some kind of training or skill. I'd never say, "Police officers have it so easy. I could do that!"

I'd never say that about any public servants. Not firefighters, sanitation workers, social workers, lawyers, doctors – even politicians.

I think most people feel the same way – except when it comes to teaching. That's the one job where everyone has an opinion and it's based on next to nothing.

Here's how it goes. *I've been a student, therefore I can be a teacher.*[122]

Imagine if we applied that logic elsewhere. *I've been sick, therefore I can be a doctor. I've been to court, therefore I can be my own lawyer. I can turn on a light, therefore I can run the electric company.*

No one would be so ignorant. Except when it comes to teaching.

But that's not all.

Not only are most folks comfortable opining about a topic of which they are so ignorant, but they feel themselves to be particular experts about one aspect of the job more than any others – summer break!

Those teachers sure have it easy, they say. *They get their summers off! That's one sweet deal!*

Don't get me wrong. As a public school teacher, I'm grateful for summer break. But it's not what non-teachers think it is.

First off, summer break is not a vacation.

When you work a regular job you get a vacation day here and there. You get a week or two of paid time off. Teachers don't get that.

During the summer teachers don't get salaried. Some of us don't even get a paycheck, and those of us that do aren't earning money for those days off. We're getting money that we already earned from August through June. This is money that was withheld from our pay during the fall and winter, money given to us now in the summer.

Wait a minute. Money withheld from our salaries? When someone pays you later for services rendered, don't they owe you interest? Usually, they do. But not for teachers.

We work for the government. We get paid with tax dollars from the community at large. If the community had to give us our salaries up front – like almost every other job in existence

– it would be harder on the taxpayers. So we let the community pay us later – interest free.

Like I said, summer break isn't a vacation. It's more like an annual couple months of being laid off.

When I say this to non-educators, though, they often smirk. "It must be pretty sweet getting so much money that you can afford to have it paid out like that."

Let me just say this – You don't know me. You don't know what the heck I can and cannot afford. Teachers aren't millionaires[123]. We're barely thousandaires. Many of us **CAN'T** afford it. We work a second job in the summer[124] – often at little more than minimum wage.

Moreover, during the school year, teaching is not a 9-5 job[125]. We don't punch a clock working 8 hours with an hour lunch and then punch out.

If I'm not at least working 10 hours a day, I'm not even trying. Those 8 hours on the books barely cover my time in front of a class of students. I get a 30-40 minute lunch, various duties throughout the day and about 40 minutes to plan what I'm going to teach. That's time to make any materials for my classes, design programs for the students, grade papers and fill out the never-ending and ever-expanding piles of paperwork.

As a language arts teacher, I routinely have my students write essays. You think they grade themselves? I've got to read those things, each and every one. I've got homework to grade. I've got scores to input into the computer. I've got parents to call, students to tutor, and a stream of detentions to oversee. And that's just the minimum, not counting any extra-curriculars, clubs, PTA meetings, meet the principal nights, etc.

So the way I see it, I'm owed a little bit of down time during the summer. I need it just to recharge my batteries. During the school year, I'm going at a pace like lightning every day. If I didn't have some time in the summer to unwind, I wouldn't be able to keep up that pace for the majority of the year.

Heck. If I'm sick one day, when I come back to school it takes a few days to get back up to speed.

But non-teachers don't know any of that, because students don't know. Students just see the teacher in class and they assume that's all we do. And that's a forgivable assumption for students. You know why? Because they're children! But you? You're an adult human being. You don't have the right to make such assumptions without any pretext at even trying to find out.

However, this is exactly what most people do. They think there's nothing wrong with complaining about teachers, especially during the summer.

And here's the worst part.

When you complain like that, you make my job so much harder.

You're going to go home with that negativity, you're going to keep voicing it, you're going to say it in front of your own impressionable children who might not seem like it, but they listen to every word you say. Not just that, but they listen to **HOW** you say it. Even more than the words, they hear the disdain.

So when school is back in session, they bring that false impression of how easy their teachers have it, and that becomes disrespect,[126] just another thing I have to overcome in order to help your child succeed.

You hear a lot in the news about foreign countries having better education systems than ours. It's mostly B.S. propaganda, playing with statistics for political ends, but there is one area where there's a grain of truth to it – respect.[127].

In many foreign countries especially in Asia[128], teachers are held in the highest esteem. It wouldn't even cross parents' minds to scorn educators, and if their kids did it, the adults would be mortally ashamed!

But not in the U.S.A. We take the one profession most dedicated to helping our children have better lives and we crap all over it.

You know that's why I'm there in the classroom – to help your child succeed. Sure I get a paycheck, but there are lots of jobs I could do to support my family, many of them paying a whole lot more while requiring less hours a week and providing actual paid vacation days.

Like most educators, I've got a master's degree. Every year I take continuing education courses. Heck! I'm even nationally board certified – a distinction of which only 112,000 teachers - about 3% of teachers throughout the country - can boast[129]. I've been nominated for teachers excellence awards. I travel across the country multiple times a year at my own expense to enrich my field. I write letters, I protest, I lobby my congress people to support our national system of public education. I've devoted my life to making a difference in young people's lives.

Isn't that something worth a little bit of respect? Don't you want someone like me to be there for your child in the classroom?

It's funny. When it comes to most public services, you wouldn't dream of denigrating a helping hand.

You'd never hear anyone say something like this:

Those damn firemen! There would be fewer fires if it weren't for them! Have you ever seen a building burning without it being surrounded by firemen? If they'd just work a little bit harder, there'd be fewer burning build-ings!

Or:

Those damn doctors! All they do is make people sick! You never see a sick person unless he's surrounded by doctors prescribing him medicines, doing surgeries. If we had fewer doctors, fewer people would get sick! Let's close more hospitals!

But this is how people talk about teachers. Regular folks have been convinced by all the propaganda that far from helping children escape ignorance, teachers actually cause it. They don't work hard enough. They don't care enough. They have too many union protections.

I've never heard anyone complain that firemen would fight fires better if they didn't have helmets and fireproof clothing. I've never heard anyone say police would work harder to fight crime if they didn't have Kevlar and service pistols.

But somehow when it comes to teachers, the situation is different.

People, you've got to understand something. We live in a world where rich folks want to take away teachers for the poor and middle class. They want your kids to learn from computer programs and YouTube while their own kids get ... teachers!

For your kids it's always narrow the curriculum, mandate more standardized tests, impose more unproven academic standards, generate more corporate profits, and demand less parental control, fewer regulations, and fewer student services.

And do you know who has volunteered to fight against all this craziness to make sure your kids actually get some kind of quality education?

THE TEACHERS!

That's right – the same people you feel empowered to deride while standing in line waiting for your burgers and fries. The same people who you have no problem denigrating with just as much certainty as ignorance.

So please, think about that next time.

Don't bitch and moan about your community's teachers. How about giving them some support?

At very least add teaching to the list of impolite topics to address in public. That's right – religion, politics **AND TEACHING**.

Because every time a non-educator vents their spleen about those lazy, no-good teachers, they make it that much easier for the powers that be to continue eroding your child's educational experience.

CHECK YOUR WALLET! YOU TOO CAN BE AN EXPERT ON TEACHER TENURE!

*It is **IMPOSSIBLE** to fire a bad teacher.*

Unless of course you document how that teacher is bad.

You know? Due process. Rights. All that liberal bullshit.

Thank goodness we have tech millionaires to stand up for the rights of totalitarians everywhere!

A slew of Microsoft wannabes is taking up the mantle of the bored rich to once again attack teacher tenure.

They claim it's almost impossible to fire bad teachers because of worker's rights.

You know who it is actually impossible to fire!? Self-appointed so-called policy experts!

No one hired them to govern our public schools. In fact, they have zero background in education. But they have oodles of cash and insufferable ennui. Somehow that makes them experts!

I wonder why no one wants to hear my pet theories on how we should organize computer systems and pay programmers. Somehow the change in my pocket doesn't qualify me to make policy at IBM, Apple or Microsoft. Strange!

But that doesn't stop millionaires and billionaires with nothing better to do than try to increase their already sky-rocketing profits.

It's disgusting. They're nothing but wealth addicts looking for a new score by stealing whatever crumbs have fallen to the floor that the rest of us need just to survive.

Time magazine[130], which decided to put this non-story on the cover for November 3, 2014, should be ashamed. But something tells me the editors couldn't care less about things like facts, truth, integrity …

After all, these are the same folks who propelled Michelle Rhee to fame on their infamous cover[131] with the then-DC-schools chief holding a broom to sweep out all the bad teach-ers. Oh! That worked out so well! Cheating scandals, anyone!?

But instead of any apology or retraction for their faulty journalism, one can imagine the following conversation at *Time's* last editorial meeting:

Editor 1: I've got a great idea for the cover! How about a bunch of know-nothing idle rich talking out of their asses!?

Editor 2: Brilliant!

I know I'm just a teacher and I don't have millions in the bank, a bulging wallet or even a platinum credit card – but let me try to draw on my more-than-a-decade of experience in the classroom to explain.

1) Tenure does not mean a job for life. It just means you have to follow due process before firing a teacher. Many other jobs have similar due process rights for their workers that they don't call tenure. Unfortunately that leads to the belief that teacher tenure is special or unique. It isn't.

2) Teachers are Evaluated Based on Student Test Scores. This is ridiculously inaccurate and unfair. Standardized tests do NOT effectively measure student learning.[132] The only thing they really measure is family income. So teachers who have richer students have generally more favorable student test scores and teacher evaluations than those who teach the poorest and most difficult children. Value-Added Measures, or VAM as these are often called, have been labeled junk science by national statistical organizations. They violate a basic principle of the field that you cannot use a test designed to evaluate one factor as a way to evaluate an entirely different factor. Removing due process would make the teachers who serve the most at-risk students unfairly at risk of losing their jobs.

3) Firing the "least effective" teachers doesn't improve education. I know this goes against common sense, but facts are facts. If you fire someone, you have to find a replacement. Ideally, you want a replacement who will do a better job than the person being removed. However, this is incredibly difficult and expensive. Half of the teachers who enter the field leave in 5 years.[133] It's a tough job that many people just can't handle. Moreover, it takes a long time to get good at it. A much more cost-effective approach is providing high-quality professional development. You can't fire yourself to the top. True, if a teacher has no interest and doesn't improve after multiple attempts to help, then it may be best for that person to seek employment elsewhere. But it's not step 1!

4) Tenure Protects the Most Experienced Teachers. Without it, veteran teachers could not compete with new hires who enter the field at a lower salary. In the long run, it costs less to keep and train veteran teachers than to hire and train new ones. But administrators and school directors often only see short-term gains. Without due process, veteran teachers would be in danger of unfair firing to increase the short-term bottom line. This would reduce the quality of education kids receive because they'd be denied the wealth of experience and talent that experienced teachers bring to the classroom.[134] Moreover, who would enter a field that only values new hires? There's no future in such a job, and it would just be a repository for a series of temps with no other choice than to teach for a few years before moving on. Teach for America, anyone?

5) Tenure Allows Teachers to Innovate. With due process, teachers can more easily make decisions based on what's best for their students and not what's politically acceptable. They don't have to give the school board director's son an "A" just because of his patronage. Kids actually have to earn their grades. And if a student doesn't like a teacher, he can't destroy the adult's career by making a baseless accusation.

But to know any of this, one would have to possess some actual information about the field. That takes knowledge and experience in education, not big money.

For some reason, the same people who are investing heavily in school privatization just can't see it. The people who champion for-profit charter schools, toxic testing and Common Core can't wrap their heads around the concept. All they see are the dollar signs of public money meant to pay for children's education being diverted into their private bank accounts.

Human suffering? Educational outcomes? Struggling students?

Who gives a shit?

Teachers do. That's why they're trying so hard to get rid of us.

NOTE: As a member of the Badass Teachers Association, I subsequently helped craft a response to the November 2014 "Time" cover that was published in "Time" magazine.[135]

THE WORST SORT OF VIOLENCE AGAINST CHILDREN

She was smiling and laughing, but her eyes were terrified.

Sitting in class among her fellow middle school students, her words were all bravado. But her gestures were wild and frightened. Tears were close.

So as the morning bell rang and the conversation continued unabated, I held myself in check. I stopped the loud rebuke forming in my teacher's throat and just listened.

"You know that shooting at Monroeville Mall Saturday night, Mr. Singer? I was there!"

I swallowed. "My gosh, Paulette. Are you okay?"

She acts street smart and unbreakable, but I can still see the little girl in her. She's only 13.

She slowed down and told us what happened, a story framed as bragging but really a desperate plea for safety and love.

She went to the mall with her mother. When they separated so she could go to the restroom, the gunfire began. She ran out and her Mom was gone. She was ushered into a nearby store where the customers were kept in lockdown. She stayed there until the police cleared the mall, and it was safe for her to find her mother and go home.

A 17-year-old boy had gunned down three people. One was his target. The others were bystanders – parents who had been unlucky enough to have gotten in the way. Now they were all in the hospital, two in critical condition.

And my student – my beautiful, precious, pain-in-the-butt, braggadocious, darling little child – was stuck in the mix.

I tried to imagine how scared she must have been separated from her mother, hiding with strangers, as police swept the shops, food court and children's play center.

Here she was telling the class her story and getting more upset with each word.

I gave her a meaningful look and told her we'd talk more later. Then I began class.

But I kept my eye on her. Was that relief I saw as the talk turned from bullets and bloodshed to similes and metaphors? Did the flush leave her cheeks as we crafted multi-paragraph theses? I hope so.

I think I know her pretty well by now. She's been mine for two years – in both 7th and 8th grades. I even taught her older brother when he was in middle school.

I know she's rarely going to do her homework – and if she does, it will be finished in the last 20 minutes. I know she'd rather be out playing volleyball or cheerleading than in school writing or reading. I know when she's secure and when she's scared.

And I know that today's lesson will be a breeze for her.

So why not put her in her comfort zone, show her that things haven't changed, that she's still the same person, that she can still do this, and that nothing is different?

At least, that was the plan.

As any experienced public school teacher knows, you have to satisfy a person's basic needs before you have any chance at teaching them something new. Psychologist Abraham Maslow's "Hierarchy of Needs" is always at the back of my mind.

Students must have their physical needs met first – be fed, have a full night's rest, etc. Then they have to feel safe, loved, and esteemed before they can reach their potentials.

But meeting these needs is a daily challenge. Our students come to us with a wealth of traumas and we're given a poverty of resources to deal with them.

How many times have I given a child breakfast or bought a lunch? How many kids were given second-hand clothes or books? How many hours have I spent before or after school just listening to a tearful child pour out his or her heart?

Let me be clear. I don't mind.

Not one bit.

It's one of the reasons I became a teacher. I **WANT** to be there for these kids. I want to be someone they can come to when they need help. It's important to me.

But what I do mind is doing this alone. And then being blamed for not healing all the years of accumulated hurt.

Because that's exactly what's expected of teachers these days. Fix this insurmountable problem with few tools and inadequate funding, and if you can't, it's your fault.

I didn't shoot up the mall. I didn't pass the laws that make it so easy for kids to get a hold of guns. I didn't pass the laws that allow such rampant income inequality and the perpetuation of crippling poverty that more than half of our nation's public school children live with every day. And I sure didn't slash public school budgets while wealthy corporations got a tax holiday.

But when society's evils are visited on our innocent children, I'm expected to handle it alone. And if I can't solve it all by myself, I should be fired.

That is where I take umbrage.

The issue is violence but not all of it comes at the end of a gun.

Keeping public schools defunded and dysfunctional is also a form of violence. Promoting school privatization and competition when kids really just need resources is also cruelty. Pretending that standardized curriculum and tests are a civil right is also savagery.

It's called class warfare. Its most prominent victims are children. Its most active soldiers are teachers. And we're on the front lines every day.

When the bell rang to end class, Paulette stopped by my desk.

I looked up at her ready to give whatever support I could. It was my lunch break, but I was willing to skip it and just talk. I'd get the guidance counselor. I'd call home. Whatever she needed.

But none of it was necessary.

"Are you okay?" I asked.

"Yeah." She gave me a big smile and a deep breath.

I returned it.

Today would be alright. Tomorrow? We'll meet that together.

But we sure could use some help.

LIFE OR DEATH PROFESSIONAL DEVELOPMENT

You know what's funny about school shootings?

It's the only time the public still universally loves teachers.

We don't trust them with collective bargaining rights. We don't think they deserve a decent salary. Heck! We don't even trust their judgement to design their own teaching standards, lead their own classrooms or be evaluated by their own principals!

But when armed assailants show up at school, then we think teachers are just great.

When angry teens arrive with rifles strapped to their trench-coated backs, carrying duffel bags full of ammunition – then teachers are heroes.

I guess you can't standardize your way past a bullet.

My school district had an outstanding training today. Administration brought in current and retired FBI agents, local law enforcement and EMTs to practice active shooter drills with the teachers.

We spent the morning learning about common factors between various school shootings, what to look for to stop the violence before it even begins, and what strategies we should consider if we're ever in such a situation.

This may sound a bit vague but the trainers asked us specifically not to give away the details. They fear if too much of this becomes common knowledge, mass shooters will be better able to prepare for their killings. So in deference to law enforcement, I'm not going to get into any specifics that might help a shooter increase his body count.

The afternoon was taken up with various scenarios. We were split into groups and given roles to play as a law enforcement officer took on the role of a school shooter.

The officer had a gun filled with blanks. We were given the opportunity to hear what it sounds like to have a gun go off in our building at various distances. It certainly wasn't what I expected, but it gave us an excellent point of reference in case the real thing ever happened.

Probably the most frightening scenarios were in our own classrooms. I was sent to the room where I teach with a group of teachers who would play the role of students. Then we practiced locking down.

When the announcement was made, I locked my door, had the "students" turn over the desks for cover and turned off the light. One of the "students" was an army veteran so he tied his leather belt to the doorknob making it harder to open.

We heard the shooter walking the halls, screaming at others, even knocking on our door and trying unsuccessfully to get inside.

However, in the very next room, he broke in causing real

damage to the door. He made the teachers kneel on the ground and asked them if they had children, if they wanted to live before shooting them with blanks.

When it was over, their faces were bloodless and scared.

During another scenario, I was only able to save one student in my room before the shooter arrived. I looked right at the shooter before slamming my door shut. There was just no time to do any more.

The two of us hid along the wall with the lights out. We even tried our army friend's belt trick but it did no good. The shooter broke through the door breaking the belt. I had my chair raised above my head and brought it down gently on his gun arm as he entered the room.

He turned to me and said "that was a good idea," before shooting me. In my defense, had this been real and not practice, I would have brought the chair down with much more force. But dead I remained until police swept the room and the scenario ended.

A friend of mine in another room said the shooter entered her classroom and asked, "Who's the teacher!?" My friend rose from the floor and said it was her. He took her outside of the room at gun point, turned her around and told her to run. She said she tried to follow his directions but her legs barely obeyed her. She doesn't remember if he shot her.

Others froze in the halls against lockers or on the floor, becoming easy targets as the shooter approached.

At one point he yelled, "Where's the principal!?" Another friend calmly gave him directions on how to get to the office. "Just go out these doors, make a left ..." But by then the principal had already run from the building. She admitted to feeling horrible after she was safe.

We did a few other scenarios where the shooter approached us in areas where there was much less cover, and we had to decide immediately what to do, where to go. It became something of a mad dash. One of the teachers even fell and broke her nose. She was treated on the scene by EMTs and taken to the hospital.

All-in-all, it was thoughtful and fascinating training. It's unfortunate we need to take the time away from academic concerns, but it is necessary. Our trainers called it "fear inoculation." They said it would help us be less frightened, more able to act if the real thing were ever to happen.

The irony is that our public schools **ARE** safe – safer even than our homes. You have a better chance of being struck by lightning than you do of being involved in a mass shooting. But these things do happen, and it's best to be prepared.

It certainly brought home the experience for me. I know what I'd do. I'd protect my students with my last breath. I think most teachers would. It's who we are.

We don't get into teaching for the salary or tenure. We certainly don't do it for the standardization, the dwindling autonomy, and the fading professional regard.

We do it for the children.

I was honored to have this article featured on Freshly Pressed[136]

THE LONGEST LASTING LESSON - A THANK YOU TO ALL THE EXCELLENT TEACHERS I'VE EVER HAD

They say teaching is the one profession that creates all the others.

That teachers affect eternity – no one can tell where their influence stops.

It's certainly true in my life.

I wouldn't be the person I am today without a string of excellent educators.

For better or worse, I am the product of decades of first-rate instruction and inspiration.

There are so many teachers who made a profound impact on my life.

Mr. Mitchell taught me how to express my opinion, and

how to listen to others and consider their point of view before responding.

Ms. Robb taught me how to organize my thoughts so they would make sense to someone else.

Mr. Geissler taught me how money and politics work together.

Ms. Neuschwander taught me the value of a good story.

And there are so many more. I wish I could remember them all.

If we're honest, everyone has had a plethora of powerful pedagogues in their lives.

Their names are legion – even if we can't remember most of them.

During one particular Teacher Appreciation Week, the one that kept popping into my head was Ms. Zadrel.

She was my third grade teacher.

I don't remember what she looked like. I don't remember most of her lessons. I'm not even sure if I'm spelling her name right.

But I do remember how she organized her class.

The room was a separate town called Zadrelville. The rows of desks were streets. Each student had a job and we earned play money.

We could send each other letters, play the lottery, vote for class mayor – almost everything you'd do in a small town. Everyday tasks were jobs – emptying the pencil sharpener, passing out papers, cleaning the blackboard, etc.

And me? I wrote the newspaper. "The News of 201" it was called.

It was a fairly gossipy rag. Headlines included things like who liked whom, if someone got paddled in gym, and which was better – Indiana Jones or Star Wars movies.

I made the paper myself, ran it off on the copier and delivered it to subscribers' desks.

I published about once a week. Any day a new edition would roll hot off the press – and it actually was warm – everyone in the class had to have one. It was essential reading.

There even may have been a few fights caused by some of my articles.

"You like Beth!? She's got cuties!"

I never got a chance to see Ms. Zadrel's lesson plans. I'm not sure exactly what she had in mind for us from this classroom management model. But I learned a lot.

Perhaps the longest lasting lesson was about myself. I learned how much I love being creative and how important it is for me to impact people's lives.

Would I have become a teacher, myself, if I hadn't had this experience? Maybe not.

I'd always enjoyed writing, but seeing such a demand for my work probably changed my life.

I wasn't just writing for **ME**. I was writing for an audience. I gauged what the class wanted from a newspaper and provided it.

My articles may have caused a stir, but no one ever unsubscribed. By putting all that everyday ephemera in one place, we all learned much more about each other.

I loved it so much that when I went to fourth grade, I kept up the paper. It didn't have quite the same magic in a class that wasn't its own self-contained city, but I'd already been bitten by the bug.

You might say that both my blog and this book are really just a continuation of that adolescent newspaper I started in Ms. Zadrel's class.

I've been a professional journalist, a freelancer and now a blogger. But I'm really just writing a classroom newspaper for people who are interested in the next edition.

Ms. Zadrel is long retired. I don't know what happened to her or if she's even still around somewhere.

I don't know what she'd say if she could read this book.

But I know what I'd say to her.

Thank you.

With all my heart – thank you.

REFERENCES

1. Harper, Aimee, Can Black People Be Racist Toward White People? June 11, 2013, *The Sistah Vegan Project* http://www.sistahvegan.com/2013/06/01/can-black-people-be-racist-towards-white-people/

2. Cole, Nicki Lisa, What's the Difference Between Prejudice and Racism? Dec. 8, 2016. *About.com* http://sociology.about.com/od/Ask-a-Sociologist/fl/Whats-the-Difference-Between-Prejudice-and-Racism.htm

3. Jones, Denisha, The Death of Michael Brown, Teachers and Racism, Aug. 18, 2014, *Badass Teachers Blog* http://badassteachers.blogspot.com/2014/08/the-death-of-michael-brown-teachers-and.html

4. Green, Laci, Is Racism Over Yet? *Laci Green's YouTube Channel*, May 8, 2015, https://www.youtube.com/watch?v=h_hx30zOi9I

5. Crosley-Corcoran, Gina, Explaining White Privilege to a Broke White Person, July 14, 2016, *Huffington Post* http://www.huffingtonpost.com/gina-crosleycorcoran/explaining-white-privilege-to-a-broke-white-person_b_5269255.html

6. Coates, Ta-Nehisi, Black People Are Not Ignoring 'Black on Black' Crime, Aug. 15, 2014, *The Atlantic* https://www.theatlantic.com/national/archive/2014/08/black-people-are-not-ignoring-black-on-black-crime/378629/

7. Du Bois, W.E.B, *Darkwater: Voices from Within the Veil*, 1920, *Project Gutenberg*. http://www.gutenberg.org/ebooks/15210?msg=welcome_stranger

8. Plessy v. Ferguson, *History.com*, http://www.history.com/topics/black-history/plessy-v-ferguson

9. 1921 Emergency Quota Law *(An act to limit the immigration of aliens into the United States)*, H.R. 4075; Pub.L. 67-5; 42 Stat. 5. 67th Congress; May 19, 1921, http://library.uwb.edu/Static/USimmigration/1921_emergency_quota_law.html

10. Jones, Brian; The Social Construction of Race; June 25, 2015; *Jacobin*; https://www.

jacobinmag.com/2015/06/racecraft-racism-social-origins-reparations/

11. Severson, Kim, Food Stamp Fraud, Rare But Troubling, Dec. 2013, *The New York Times*, http://www.nytimes.com/2013/12/19/us/food-stamp-fraud-in-the-underground-economy.html?_r=0

12. The Daily Take Team, The Thom Hartmann Program. Food Stamps Are Affordable - Corporate Welfare Is Not, Nov. 2013, *Truth-Out*; http://www.truth-out.org/opinion/item/19844-food-stamps-are-affordable-corporate-welfare-is-not

13. Buchheit, Paul, Add it Up: The Average American Family Pays $6,000 a Year on Subsidies to Big Business, Sept. 2013, *CommonDreams.org*, https://www.commondreams.org/views/2013/09/23/add-it-average-american-family-pays-6000-year-subsidies-big-business

14. Freire, Paulo, *Pedagogy of the Oppressed*, 1968, Bloomsbury

15. Paxton, Tom, *What Did You learn In School Today*, AZlyrics, http://www.azlyrics.com/lyrics/tompaxton/whatdidyoulearninschooltoday.html

16. Snopes, http://www.snopes.com/racial/language/le-a.asp

17. Key & Peele, *Comedy Central*, http://www.cc.com/video-clips/w5hxki/key-and-peele-substitute-teacher-pt--1 http://www.cc.com/video-clips/ohi0y3/key-and-peele-substitute-teacher-pt--2

18. Fryer, Roland; Levitt, Steven, The Causes and Consequences of Distinctively Black Names, Aug. 2004, *The Quarterly Journal of Economics*, http://www.jstor.org/stable/25098702?&seq=1#page_scan_tab_contents

19. Berkshire, Jennifer, Backpacks Full of Cash, July 2015, *Edushyster*, http://havey-ouheardblog.com/backpacks-full-of-cash/

20. Lecker, Wendy, School Choice, or Extortion?, Nov. 2013, *Stamford Advocate*, http://www.stamfordadvocate.com/news/article/Lecker-School-choice-or-extortion-5022275.php

21. Clawson, Laura, Nashville Charter Schools 'Lose' Problem Students to Public Schools-Just in Time for Testing, May 21, 2013, *Daily Kos* http://www.dailykos.com/story/2013/05/21/1210512/-Nashville-charter-schools-lose-problem-students-to-public-schools-just-in-time-for-testing

22. Weber, Mark, Charters That Kick Out Kids Have NOTHING to Teach Real Public Schools, Aug. 8, 2013, *Jersey Jazzman*, http://jerseyjazzman.blogspot.com/2013/08/charters-that-kick-out-kids-have.html

23. Rawls, Kristin, The Ugly Truth About 'School Choice', Jan. 24, 2012, *Alternet* http://www.salon.com/2012/01/24/the_ugly_truth_about_school_choice/

24. Multiple Choice: Charter School Performance in 16 States, 2009, *Center for Research on Education Outcomes* http://credo.stanford.edu/reports/MULTIPLE_CHOICE_CREDO.pdf

25. Herold, Benjamin, Cyber Charters Have 'Overwhelming Negative Impact', CREDO Study Finds, Oct. 2015, *Education Week*, http://blogs.edweek.org/edweek/DigitalEducation/2015/10/CREDO_online_charters_study.html

26. Choice Without Equity: Charter School Segregation and the Need for Civil Rights Standards, 2009, *The Civil Rights Project* https://www.civilrightsproject. ucla.edu/research/k-12-education/integration-and-diversity/choice-without-equity-2009-report

27. Strauss, Valerie, The Link Between Charter School Expansion and Increasing Segregation, March 2014, *The Washington Post*, https://www.washingtonpost.com/news/answer-sheet/wp/2014/03/13/the-link-between-charter-school-expansion-and-increasing-segregation/?utm_term=.b18c8132006a

28. Greene, Peter, School choice and Disenfranchising the Public, March 7, 2015, *Huffington Post*, http://www.huffingtonpost.com/peter-greene/school-choice-and-disenfranchising-the-public_b_6420248.html

29. Kasperkevic, Jana, More Than Half of US Public School Students Live in Poverty, Report Finds, Jan. 17, 2015, *The Guardian*, https://www.theguardian.com/money/us-money-blog/2015/jan/17/public-school-students-poverty-report

30. Cardinali, Daniel, How to Get Kids to Class: To Keep Poor Students in School, Provide Social Services, Aug. 25, 2014, *The New York Times*, https://www.nytimes.com/2014/08/26/opinion/to-keep-poor-kids-in-school-provide-social-services.html?_r=0

31. Schneider, Mercedes, Diane Ravitch's Realistic Assessment of 2013 NAEP Results and Reform 'Success', November, 2013, *Huffington Post*, http://www.huffingtonpost.com/mercedes-schneider/ravitchs-realistic-assess_b_4289793.html

32. Strauss, Valerie, Why Schools Aren't Businesses: The Blueberry Story, July 2013, *The Washington Post*, https://www.washingtonpost.com/news/answer-sheet/wp/2013/07/09/why-schools-arent-businesses-the-blueberry-story/?utm_term=.d66620d3498b

33. Wermund, Benjamin, Vouchers Have Been a Tough Sell When Put to a Vote, Dec. 2016, *Politico*, http://www.politico.com/tipsheets/morning-education/2016/12/vouchers-have-been-a-tough-sell-when-put-to-a-vote-217673

34. Fischer, Brendan, Lobbying Powerhouse ALEC Pushed 172 School Privatization Bills Last Year, March 2016, *PR Watch*, http://www.alternet.org/education/cashing-kids-corporate-lobbying-powerhouse-alec-pushed-172-school-privatization-bills-last

35. Strauss, Valerie, Obama's Real Education Legacy: Common Core, Testing, Charter Schools, Oct. 2016, *The Washington Post*, https://www.washingtonpost.com/news/answer-sheet/wp/2016/10/21/obamas-real-education-legacy-common-core-testing-charter-schools/?utm_term=.b6a22596bc23

36. Bonastia, Christopher, The Racist History of the Charter School Movement, Jan. 2015, *Alternet*, http://www.alternet.org/education/racist-history-charter-school-movement

37. Williams, Yohuru, With Public Schools Under Attack, What Would Martin Say?, Jan. 2015, *The Progressive*, https://www.commondreams.org/views/2015/01/18/public-schools-under-attack-what-would-martin-say

38. Wilson, Bruce, How School Privatization Was Hatched by Racist 1950s Southern

Segregationists, Oct. 2013, _Alternet_, http://www.alternet.org/speakeasy/brucewilson/how-school-privatization-was-hatched-racist-1950s-southern-segregationists

39. Toppo, Greg, GAO Study: Segregation Worsening in U.S. Schools, May 2016, _USA Today_, https://www.usatoday.com/story/news/2016/05/17/gao-study-segregation-worsening-us-schools/84508438/

40. Tabachnick, Rachel; The 'Christian' Dogma Pushed by Religious Schools That Are Supported by Your Tax Dollars, May 23, 2011, _Alternet_, http://www.alternet.org/story/151046/the_%27christian%27_dogma_pushed_by_religious_schools_that_are_supported_by_your_tax_dollars

41. Pan, Deanna, 14 Wacky 'Facts' Kids Will Learn in Louisiana's Voucher Schools, Aug. 2012, _Mother Jones_, http://www.motherjones.com/kevin-drum/2012/08/photos-evangelical-curricula-louisiana-tax-dollars/

42. Davis, Carl, How States Turn K-12 Scholarships Into Money-Laundering Schemes, March 2017, _The American Prospect_, http://www.alternet.org/education/how-states-turn-k-12-scholarships-money-laundering-schemes

43. Herzenberg, Stephen; Tabachnik, Rachel, Still No Accountability with Taxpayer-Funded Vouchers for Private and Religious School Tuition, April 2017, _Pennsylvania Budget and Policy Center_, http://www.pennbpc.org/still-no-accountability, www.pennbpc.org/sites/pennbpc.org/files/20170405_PA%20OSTC-EITC.pdf

44. Perez-Pena, Richard, Contrary to Trump's Claims, Immigrants Are Less Likely to Commit Crimes, Jan. 2017, _The New York Times_, https://www.nytimes.com/2017/01/26/us/trump-illegal-immigrants-crime.html?_r=0

45. Patel, Jugal; Andrews, Wilson; Trump's Electoral College Victory Ranks 46th in 58 Elections, Dec. 2016, _The New York Times_, https://www.nytimes.com/interactive/2016/12/18/us/elections/donald-trump-electoral-college-popular-vote.html

46. Ravitch, Diane; Obama's Education Reform Push is Bad Education Policy, March 2010, _The Los Angeles Times_, https://www.commondreams.org/news/2010/03/14/obamas-education-reform-push-bad-education-policy

47. McCandless, David, Common Myth Conceptions, Sept. 2014, _informationisbeautiful.net_ http://www.informationisbeautiful.net/visualizations/common-mythconceptions-worlds-most-contagious-falsehoods/

48. Baeder, Justin, Why U.S. Schools Are Simply the Best, Oct. 22, 2012, _Education Week_, http://blogs.edweek.org/edweek/on_performance/2012/10/why_us_schools_are_simply_the_best.html

49. Scommegna, Paola, U.S. Growing Bigger, Older and More Diverse, April 2004, _Population Reference Bureau_ http://www.prb.org/Publications/Articles/2004/USGrowingBiggerOlderandMoreDiverse.aspx

50. Farhi, Paul; Flunking the Test, April/May 2012, _American Journalism Review_, http://ajrarchive.org/Article.asp?id=5280

51. National Center for Education Statistics, 2015, https://nces.ed.gov/timss/

52. Ravitch, Diane, My View of the PISA Scores, Sept. 3, 2013, _DianeRavitch.net_ https://dianeravitch.net/2013/12/03/my-view-of-the-pisa-scores/

53. Robinson, Mitchell, The One About Data, Numbers and Truth, June, 13, 2015, *mitchellrobinson.net* https://www.mitchellrobinson.net/2015/06/13/the-one-about-data-numbers-and-truth/

54. Porter, Eduardo, School vs. Society in America's Failing Students, Nov. 3, 2015, *The New York Times* https://www.nytimes.com/2015/11/04/business/economy/school-vs-society-in-americas-failing-students.html?_r=1

55. Porter, Eduardo, Education Gap Between Rich and Poor is Growing Wider, Sept. 22, 2015, *The New York Times* https://www.nytimes.com/2015/09/23/business/economy/education-gap-between-rich-and-poor-is-growing-wider.html

56. Carnoy, Martin; Garcia, Emma; Khavenson, Tatiana, Bringing It Back Home, Oct. 20, 2015, *Economic Policy Institute*, http://www.epi.org/publication/bringing-it-back-home-why-state-comparisons-are-more-useful-than-international-comparisons-for-improving-u-s-education-policy/

57. Greenhalgh, Simon, The Hidden Costs of Asia's High Test Scores, Dec. 9, 2016, *The Diplomat*, http://thediplomat.com/2016/12/the-hidden-costs-of-asias-high-test-scores/

58. LaFee, Scott; Zhao: Diversity and Creativity Benefit U.S. Public Schools, *The School Superintendents Association* http://www.aasa.org/content.aspx?id=27308

59. Tatlow, Didi Kirsten, Q. and A.: Yong Zhao on Education and Authoritarian-ism in China, Sept. 14, 2014, *Sinosphere: Dispatches From China; The New York Times*, https://sinosphere.blogs.nytimes.com/2014/09/14/q-and-a-yong-zhao-on-education-and-authoritarianism-in-china/

60. Knapp, Bill, Middle Class is Moving Forward, Not Backward, Jan. 15, 2012, *The Washington Post* https://www.washingtonpost.com/opinions/middle-class-is-moving-forward-not-backward/2012/01/13/gIQAJmhn1P_story.html?utm_term=.14fda5cd8243

61. Gewertz, Catherine; Record U.S. Graduation Rate Not Seen as Inflated, May 2017, *Education Week,* http://www.edweek.org/ew/articles/2017/05/10/record-us-graduation-rate-not-seen-as.html

62. Lopez, Shane, Parents, Americans Much More Positive About Local Schools, Aug. 19, 2011, *Gallup* http://www.gallup.com/poll/149093/parents-americans-positive-local-schools.aspx

63. Ravitch, Diane, Public Education: Who Are the Corporate Reformers? March 28, 2014, *Moyers and Company* http://billmoyers.com/2014/03/28/public-education-who-are-the-corporate-reformers/

64. Rapoport, Abby, Education Inc.: How Private Companies Profit from Public Schools, Sept. 8, 2011, *The Texas Observer* http://www.commondreams.org/views/2011/09/08/education-inc-how-private-companies-profit-public-schools

65. Farhi, Paul, Flunking the Test, May 2012, *The Washington Post* http://ajrarchive.org/Article.asp?id=5280

66. When You See Pro-Testing Statements From Civil Rights Organizations & Lead-ers, Check Their Gates Foundation Links, April 2015, *Perdido Street School*, http://perdidostreetschool.blogspot.com/2015/04/when-you-see-pro-testing-

statements.html

67. Darling-Hammond, Linda, 'Test-And-Punish' Sabotages Quality of Children's Education, April 2013, *Stanford Center for Opportunity Policy in Education*, https://edpolicy.stanford.edu/blog/entry/753

68. Stoskopf, Alan, The Forgotten History of Eugenics, March 2003, *Rethinking Schools*, https://www.rethinkingschools.org/articles/the-forgotten-history-of-eugenics

69. Hagopian, Jesse, 'Occupy Education' Debates the Gates Foundation (and Wins), March 2012, *Common Dreams*, https://www.commondreams.org/views/2012/03/13/occupy-education-debates-gates-foundation-and-wins

70. Knefel, Molly Jane, How Standardized Testing Reveals Stark Inequalities Between Rich and Poor, May 2015, *Alternet*, http://www.alternet.org/education/how-standardized-testing-reveals-stark-inequalities-between-rich-and-poor

71. Gil-White, Francisco, Resurrecting Racism: The Modern Attack on Black People Using Phony *Science*, 2004, Chapter 8, http://www.hirhome.com/rr/rrchap8.htm

72. Yerkes, Robert, Introduction; Brigham, Carl, *Study of American Intelligence*, 1922, Princeton University Press, http://www.archive.org/stream/studyofamericani-00briguoft/studyofamericani00briguoft_djvu

73. Jaschik, Scott, New Evidence of Racial Bias on SAT, June 2010, *Inside Higher Ed*, https://www.insidehighered.com/news/2010/06/21/sat

74. Terman, Lewis, *The Measure of Intelligence*, 1916, Boston: Houghton Mifflin, http://www.gutenberg.org/ebooks/20662?msg=welcome_stranger

75. Hitler, Adolph, *Mein Kampf*, 1925, Eher Verlag, http://www.hitler.org/writings/Mein_Kampf/

76. Riggs, Ransom, The Frightening History of Eugenics in America, Feb. 2011, *Mental Floss*, http://mentalfloss.com/article/27029/frightening-history-eugenics-america

77. Black, Edwin, Hitler's Debt to America, Feb. 2004, *The Guardian*, https://www.theguardian.com/uk/2004/feb/06/race.usa

78. Black, Edwin, The Horrifying American Roots of Nazi Eugenics, 2003, *Dialog Press*, http://historynewsnetwork.org/article/1796

79. Cohen, Adam, Buck v. Bell: Inside the SCOTUS Case That Led to Forced Sterilization of 70,000 & Inspired the Nazis, March 2016, *Democracy Now*, https://www.democracynow.org/2016/3/17/buck_v_bell_inside_the_scotus

80. Begos, Kevin, The American Eugenics Movement After World War II, May 2011, *Indy Week*, https://www.indyweek.com/indyweek/the-american-eugenics-movement-after-world-war-ii-part-1-of-3/Content?oid=2468789

81. Paton, Dean, The Myth Behind Public School Failure, Feb. 2014, *Yes! Magazine*, http://www.yesmagazine.org/issues/education-uprising/the-myth-behind-public-school-failure

82. Vasquez Heilig, Julian, A Top Ten of @ArneDuncan Inanity: Obama's Basketball Buddy Drops Ball on Ed, Nov. 2013, *Cloaking Inequity*, https://cloakinginequity.

com/2013/11/18/a-top-ten-of-duncans-inanity-obamas-basketball-buddy-drops-ball-on-ed/

83. Loewen, James, Here We Go Again: Tests for the Common Core May Be Unfair to Some and Boring to All, Nov. 2014, *History News Network*, http://historynews-network.org/blog/153543

84. Anderson, Nick, Education Secretary Duncan calls Hurricane Katrina good for New Orleans schools, January 30, 2010, *The Washington Post* http://www.wash-ingtonpost.com/wp-dyn/content/article/2010/01/29/AR2010012903259.html

85. Berkshire, Jennifer, 'Reform' Makes Broken New Orleans Schools Worse: Race, Charters, Testing and the Real Story of Education After Katrina, Aug. 2015, *Salon*, http://www.salon.com/2015/08/03/reform_makes_broken_new_orleans_schools_worse_race_charters_testing_and_the_real_story_of_education_after_katrina/

86. Layton, Lyndsey, Charters Not Outperforming Nation's Traditional Public Schools, Report Says, June 2013, *The Washington Post*, https://www.washingtonpost.com/local/education/charters-not-outperforming-nations-traditional-public-schools-report-says/2013/06/24/23f19bb8-dd0c-11e2-bd83-e99e43c336ed_story.html?utm_term=.cc66c41b43e8

87. Figueroa, Alyssa, 8 Things You Should Know About Corporations Like Pearson That Make Huge Profits from Standardized Tests, Aug 2013, *Alternet*, http://www.alternet.org/education/corporations-profit-standardized-tests

88. Walsh, Russ, Dump Dibels, March 2015, *Russ on Reading*, http://russonreading.blogspot.com/2015/03/dump-dibels.html

89. Strauss, Valerie, Murdoch Buys Education Technology Company, Nov. 2010, *The Washington Post,* http://voices.washingtonpost.com/answer-sheet/murdoch-buys-education-technol.html

90. DIBELS Raises Common Core Cut Scores to Show More Students Below Grade Level, Feb. 2015, *Lace to the Top*, https://lacetothetop.wordpress.com/2015/02/13/dibels-raises-common-core-cut-scores-to-show-more-students-below-grade-level/comment-page-1/#comment-241

91. Greene, Peter, Selling Competency-Based Education, Nov. 2016, *Huffington Post*, http://www.huffingtonpost.com/peter-greene/selling-competency-based-education_b_8598450.html

92. Competency Based-Ed- the Culmination of the Common Core Agenda, Nov. 2015, *Stop Common Core NYS*, https://stopcommoncorenys.wordpress.com/2015/11/03/competency-based-ed-the-culmination-of-the-common-core-agenda/

93. Cody, Anthony, Will Competency-Based Learning Rescue the Testocracy?, Nov. 2015, *Living in Dialogue*, http://www.livingindialogue.com/will-competency-based-learning-rescue-the-testocracy/

94. Schneider, Mercedes, Those 24 Common Core 2009 Work Group Members, April 2014, *Deutsch29*, https://deutsch29.wordpress.com/2014/04/23/those-24-common-core-2009-work-group-members/

95. Darling-Hammond, Linda, Teachers Paid Much Less Than Their Peers, Nov. 2011, *US News and World Report*, https://www.usnews.com/debate-club/are-teachers-

overpaid/teachers-paid-much-less-than-their-peers

96. Kohn, Alfie, The Overselling of Ed Tech, March 2016, *alfiekohn.org*, http://www. alfiekohn.org/blogs/ed-tech/

97. Summers, Juana, Kids and Screen Time: What Does the Research Say?, Aug. 2014, *NPR*, http://www.npr.org/sections/ed/2014/08/28/343735856/kids-and-screen-time-what-does-the-research-say

98. Greene, Peter, What's So Bad About Competency Based Education?, March 2014, *Curmudgucation*, http://curmudgucation.blogspot.com/2016/03/whats-so-bad-about-competency-based.html

99. Talmage, Emily, Five Secrets of CBE Salesmen, Nov. 2015, *emilytalmage.com*, https://emilytalmage.com/2015/11/12/five-secrets-of-cbe-salesmen/

100. Jacobs, Joanne, Why Teachers Hate 'Close Reading', Aug. 2014, *Linking and Thinking on Education*, http://www.joannejacobs.com/2014/08/why-teachers-hate-close-reading/

101. Cody, Anthony, Common Core Close Reading Comes to California, Jan. 2014, *Living in Dialogue*, http://blogs.edweek.org/teachers/living-in-dialogue/2014/01/common_core_close_reading_come.html

102. Greene, Peter, Why Did the Core Have a Bad Year?, Aug. 2014, *Curmudgucation*, http://curmudgucation.blogspot.com/2014/08/why-did-core-have-bad-year.html

103. Yatvin, Joanne, What the Dickens is the Common Core Doing?, Dec. 2015, *The Treasure Hunter*, https://joanneyatvin.org/2015/12/05/what-the-dickens-is-the-common-core-doing/

104. Owens, Eric, Bill Gates Loves Common Core for Your Kids, BUT NOT HIS, March 2014, *Daily Caller*, http://dailycaller.com/2014/03/23/bill-gates-wants-to-force-common-core-on-your-kids-but-leave-his-kids-out-of-it/

105. Wong, Alia, When Parents Are the Ones Getting Schooled by the Common Core, Aug. 2015, *The Atlantic*, https://www.theatlantic.com/education/archive/2015/08/common-core-schools-parents/400559/

106. Engel, Pamela, Why Parents Hate Common Core Math, July 2014, *Business Insider*, http://www.slate.com/blogs/business_insider/2014/07/10/common_core_math_questions_show_why_parents_are_upset_about_its_methods.html

107. Strauss, Valerie, Common Core: the Gift That Pearson Counts on to Keep Giving, Sept. 2015, *The Washington Post*, https://www.washingtonpost.com/news/answer-sheet/wp/2015/09/23/common-core-the-gift-that-pearson-counts-on-to-keep-giving/?utm_term=.8eeef65f8b72

108. Hart, Shane Vander, Debunking Misconceptions: 'The Common Core is State-Led', Jan. 2013, *Truth in American Education*, https://truthinamericaneducation.com/common-core-state-standards/debunking-misconceptions-the-common-core-is-state-led/

109. Stoltzfoos, Rachel, Is Common Core State-Led? March 2014, *Daily Caller*, http://dailycaller.com/2014/03/17/is-common-core-state-led/#ixzz47sfJQQsn

110. Pullmann, Joy, Ten Common Core Promoters Laughing All the Way to the Bank,

Jan. 2015, *The Federalist*, http://thefederalist.com/2015/01/05/ten-common-core-promoters-laughing-all-the-way-to-the-bank/

111. Stotsky, Sandra, Fact Sheet on Common Core's Developers, Writers, Validation Committee, and Standards, March 2014, *uaedreform.org*, http://www.uaedreform.org/downloads/2014/03/fact-sheet-on-common-cores-developers-writers-validation-committee-and-standards.pdf

112. Ravitch, Diane, Everything You Need to Know About Common Core, Jan. 2014, *The Washington Post*, https://www.washingtonpost.com/news/answer-sheet/wp/2014/01/18/everything-you-need-to-know-about-common-core-ravitch/?utm_term=.d7b775fb3b85

113. Evers, Williamson, The Common-Core Standards' Undemocratic Push, Jan. 2015, *Education Week*, http://www.edweek.org/ew/articles/2015/01/14/the-standards-undemocratic-push.html

114. Cody, Anthony, Common Core PR Offensive Rewrites History to Ignore Failures, Aug. 2015, *Living in Dialogue*, http://www.livingindialogue.com/common-core-pr-offensive-rewrites-history-to-ignore-failures/

115. Layton, Lyndsey, How Bill Gates Pulled Off the Swift Common Core Revolution, June 2014, *The Washington Post*, https://www.washingtonpost.com/politics/how-bill-gates-pulled-off-the-swift-common-core-revolution/2014/06/07/a830e32e-ec34-11e3-9f5c-9075d5508f0a_story.html?utm_term=.248c4649d800

116. Hiller, Robin; Cody, Anthony; A Poison Pill for Learning, Sept. 2014, *U.S. News and World Report*, https://www.usnews.com/opinion/articles/2014/09/02/the-common-core-standards-are-bad-for-teachers

117. Tully, Sarah, National Poll Shows Majority Oppose Common Core Standards, Aug. 2015, *EdSource*, https://edsource.org/2015/national-poll-shows-most-oppose-common-core-standards/85212

118. No Art Left Behind, *Living in Dialogue*, http://www.livingindialogue.com/no-art-left-behind-introducing-a-new-series/

119. Thank a Union: 36 Ways Unions Have Improved Your Life, May 2012, *Daily Kos*, https://www.dailykos.com/story/2012/05/16/1092027/-Thanks-a-Union-36-Ways-Unions-Have-Improved-Your-Life

120. Greenhouse, Steven, Share of the Work Force in a Union Falls to a 97-Year Low, 11.3%; Jan. 2013, *The New York Times*, http://www.nytimes.com/2013/01/24/business/union-membership-drops-despite-job-growth.html?_r=0

121. Greenhouse, Steven, Our Economic Pickle, Jan. 2013, *The New York Times*, http://www.nytimes.com/2013/01/13/sunday-review/americas-productivity-climbs-but-wages-stagnate.html

122. Blaine, Sarah, The Teachers, Feb. 2014, *Parenting the Core*, https://parentingthecore.com/2014/02/18/the-teachers/

123. Rampell, Catherine, Teacher Pay Around the World, Sept. 2009, *The New York Times*, https://economix.blogs.nytimes.com/2009/09/09/teacher-pay-around-the-world/?_r=0

124. Martin, Carmel, School is Never Out for Teachers, July 2015, *U.S. News and World Report*, https://www.usnews.com/opinion/knowledge-bank/2015/07/15/school-is-out-but-teachers-are-still-working

125. Klein, Rebecca, American Teachers Spend More Time In The Classroom Than World Peers, Says Report, Sept. 2014, *Huffington Post*, http://www.huffingtonpost.com/2014/09/09/oecd-teacher-salary-report_n_5791166.html

126. Ryan, Julia, Poll: Teachers Don't Get No Respect, Jan. 2014, *The Atlantic*, https://www.theatlantic.com/education/archive/2014/01/poll-teachers-dont-get-no-respect/283318/

127. Dolton, Peter, Why Do Some Countries Respect Their Teachers More Than Others?, Oct. 2013, *The Guardian*, https://www.theguardian.com/teacher-network/teacher-blog/2013/oct/03/teacher-respect-status-global-survey

128. Coughlan, Sean, Teachers in China Given Highest Level of Public Respect, Oct. 2013, *BBC News*, http://www.bbc.com/news/education-24381946

129. National Board for Professional Teaching Standards http://www.nbpts.org/national-board-certification/

130. Edwards, Haley Sweetland, The War on Teacher Tenure, Oct. 2014, *Time Magazine*, http://time.com/3533556/the-war-on-teacher-tenure/

131. Strauss, Valerie, Is it Time to Kiss Michelle Rhee Goodbye?, May 2013, *The Washington Post*, https://www.washingtonpost.com/news/answer-sheet/wp/2013/05/19/is-it-time-to-kiss-michelle-rhee-goodbye/?utm_term=.fad512a1995c

132. Popham, W. James, Why Standardized Tests Don't Measure Educational Quality, March 1999, *Using Standards and Assessments*, http://www.ascd.org/publications/educational-leadership/mar99/vol56/num06/Why-Standardized-Tests-Don%27t-Measure-Educational-Quality.aspx

133. Seidel, Aly, The Teacher Dropout Crisis, July 2014, *NPR*, http://www.npr.org/sections/ed/2014/07/18/332343240/the-teacher-dropout-crisis

134. Ladd, Helen F., Why Experienced Teachers Are Important – and What Can Be Done to Develop Them, Nov. 2013, *Scholars Strategy Network*, http://www.scholarsstrategynetwork.org/sites/default/files/ssn_basic_facts_ladd_on_the_importance_of_experienced_teacgers_1.pdf

135. Kilfoyle, Marla; Tomlinson, Melissa; Singer, Steven; Williams, Yohuru; Badass Teachers Association Responds to TIME Cover, Oct. 2014, *Time* magazine, http://time.com/3541411/bats-time-cover/

136. Freshly Pressed - https://wordpress.com/discover

ABOUT THE AUTHOR

STEVEN SINGER

Steven Singer is an 8th grade Language Arts teacher in western Pennsylvania. He is a National Board Certified Teacher and has an MAT from the University of Pittsburgh.

He is Director of the Research and Blogging Committee for the Badass Teachers Association, and is co-founder of the Pennsylvania-based education budget advocacy group T.E.A.C.H. (Tell Everyone All Cuts Hurt). He ran a successful campaign through Moveon.org against the since repealed Voter ID law in the Keystone State. He joined United Opt Out as an administrator in 2016. He is a member of the Education Bloggers Network.

His writing on education and civil rights issues has appeared in the Washington Post, Education Week, the LA Progressive, Commondreams.org, Portside Navigator and has been featured on Diane Ravitch's site. He blogs at gadflyonthewallblog. wordpress.com.